D0943010

A Kabbalistic Handbook
for the Practicing Magician

OTHER TITLES FROM NEW FALCON PUBLICATIONS

Ceremonial Magic & the Power of Evocation
Kabbalistic Cycles & the Mastery of Life
    By Joseph C. Lisiewski, Ph.D.
Cosmic Trigger: Final Secret of the Illuminati
Prometheus Rising
    By Robert Anton Wilson
Undoing Yourself With Energized Meditation
Techniques for Undoing Yourself Audio CDs
The Psychopath's Bible
    By Christopher S. Hyatt, Ph.D.
Rebels & Devils: The Psychology of Liberation
    Edited by Christopher S. Hyatt, Ph.D. with contributions by
    Wm. S. Burroughs, Timothy Leary, Robert Anton Wilson et al.
Pacts With the Devil: A Chronicle of Sex, Blasphemy & Liberation
Urban Voodoo: A Beginner's Guide to Afro-Caribbean Magic
    By S. Jason Black and Christopher S. Hyatt, Ph.D.
Taboo: Sex, Religion & Magick
The Enochian World of Aleister Crowley: Enochian Sex Magic
    By Christopher S. Hyatt, Ph.D., Lon Milo DuQuette, et al.
Info-Psychology
Neuropolitique
    By Timothy Leary, Ph.D.
Condensed Chaos: An Introduction to Chaos Magick
Prime Chaos: Adventures in Chaos Magick
The Pseudonomicon
    By Phil Hine
PsyberMagick
The Chaos Magick Audio CDs
    By Peter Carroll
The Complete Golden Dawn System of Magic
The Golden Dawn Audio CDs
    By Israel Regardie
Monsters & Magical Sticks: There's No Such Thing As Hypnosis?
    By Steven Heller
Astrology & Consciousness
    By Rio Olesky
Astrology, Aleister & Aeon
    By Charles Kipp

**For the latest information on availability and prices,
please visit our website at http://www.newfalcon.com**

A KABBALISTIC HANDBOOK
FOR THE
PRACTICING MAGICIAN

A Course in the Theory and Practice of
Western Magic

by

Joseph C. Lisiewski, Ph.D.

NEW FALCON PUBLICATIONS
TEMPE, ARIZONA, U.S.A.

Copyright © 2005 by Joseph C. Lisiewski, Ph.D.

All rights reserved. No part of this book, in part or in whole, may be reproduced, transmitted, or utilized, in any form or by any means, electronic or mechanical, including photocopying, recording, or by any information storage and retrieval system, without permission in writing from the publisher, except for brief quotations in critical articles, books and reviews.

International Standard Book Number: 1-56184-236-2
Library of Congress Catalog Card Number: 2005930906

First Edition 2005

This story is based on true events. Names and locations have been changed when necessary to protect the identity of the participants.

Cover by Linda Joyce Franks

The paper used in this publication meets the minimum requirements of the American National Standard for Permanence of Paper for Printed Library Materials Z39.48-1984

Address all inquiries to:
NEW FALCON PUBLICATIONS
1739 East Broadway Road #1-277
Tempe, AZ 85282 U.S.A.
(or)
320 East Charleston Blvd. #204-286
Las Vegas, NV 89104 U.S.A.

**website: http://www.newfalcon.com
email: info@newfalcon.com**

Dedication

To Christopher S. Hyatt, Ph.D., my dearest and oldest friend in Magic, the Occult, and so very much more. Throughout the decades, Chris, your council, support, friendship, and instruction have been—and always will be—of priceless value to me.

And to the two greatest Teachers with whom the Gods have blessed me—Francis Israel Regardie and Frater Albertus. Without their Teachings and kindness, my work in these matters would never have grown, and would not have come to light.

Table of Contents

Illustrations

To The Reader

For the Theurgist or practicing Magician of nearly any system of Magic extant, there is no more crucial working knowledge than that of Kabbalah. This complex theological, philosophical, and theosophical structure serves not only as the backdrop against which the magician's thoughts, ideas, ritual, and ceremonial performances are placed, but it is also a living force that breaths life into one's secret occult practices.

Kabbalah is the font and wellspring from which the magician draws the necessary intellectual, emotional, and psychic energy that *first* through study and mental assimilation, and *later* through magical practice, becomes integrated into the practitioner's subconscious state of Subjective Synthesis. This process of assimilation and practice does not simply allow the magic to work: it is the mechanism that actually *causes* the magic to produce the desired effects.

Despite the numerous books on 'Qabalah' available today, and the various Encyclopedias and Cyclopedias that have appeared on the subject, none of them seem to give those johnny-on-the-spot attributions, correspondences, and key concepts in a user-friendly style that allows for immediate access. That is, not until now.

In this *Kabbalistic Handbook for the Practicing Magician*, I have attempted to cut through the red tape of lengthy, preliminary, artificial, proprietary knowledge that has come to typify those Kabbalistic elements that are more often than not either not needed by the Goetiaist, Magician, or Theurgist for his or her *immediate* work, or which otherwise are unavailable at a moment's notice.

Rather than wade through the voluminous chapters of many different books on the subject, I have tried to insure that the Kabbalistic knowledge the practitioner needs at any given instant—and depending upon the type or branch of magic being engaged in—can be easily located in this uniquely structured and formatted book on Kabbalah. By providing this information, doubt and error are thus eliminated and valuable time is saved, clearing the field for the practitioner's main objective, which is the realization of his or her wants and desires, manifested for all to see, through properly executed ritual and ceremonial work.

This said, it may be that readers acquainted with my two earlier efforts, *Ceremonial Magic and the Power of Evocation*[1], and *Kabbalistic Cycles and the Mastery of Life*[2], might raise the objection as to why this book is being written for today's practicing magician. Clearly, current day magicians almost exclusively practice some form of Golden Dawn Magic, Crowley-based Magic, or any number of variations of their offshoots, all of which can most certainly be dubbed as being "New Age."

You might be saying, isn't this the same author who spent so much time downgrading the New Age and its contemporary ritualistic foundation in his earlier books? You might wonder what I am up to, or indeed, if this present book represents some type of turnaround for me. Maybe I am trying to creep quietly back into mainstream modern magic? Or perhaps I'm simply looking for new material to write more books, hoping no one will notice my change of heart?

Let me put the reader's mind at ease, and answer these questions in a sequence that I trust will make sense. First of all, I make no apologies for any cutting remarks about the New Age and its brand of so-called Magic, or Magick, if you prefer. My opinions of the bulk of clap-trap out there that cloaks itself in the guise of the New Age, still stands and it will not change. Forty years of working within its artificial boundaries of intellectual vagaries and theoretical hedging, imbalanced 'systems,' and outright incorrect and therefore dangerous practices, have taught me all I need to know about the New Age and its myriad forms of ramblings.

As I have stressed before, the ritualistic and ceremonial practices that are designated as Modern Magic(k) are in one form or another either directly founded upon, or extrapolated from any number of earlier Hermetic, Dark Ages, Medieval, Renaissance, or Transition Era systems of magical thought, whether contemporary books on the subject admit to it or not. This is true whether these present day books carry the name of Golden Dawn, or what have you.

Because of this fact, even though my primary personal magical involvement is in Old System (Medieval and Renaissance Magic) as defined in my earlier title on Ceremonial Magic, neither I nor any other serious student of magic are therefore excluded from engaging in ritual performances that are currently attributed to the so-called New Age. But maybe this statement sounds like I am talking in circles. The answer to any doubt that may still linger in the reader's mind is simplicity itself, so allow me to elaborate a bit further on this matter.

As I have pointed out on earlier occasions, New Age material has by and large been derived directly from the grimoires (Grammars of magic) of the Old System of magic, primarily from *Three Books of Occult Philosophy*, and *Fourth Book of Occult Philosophy*,[3,4] both attributed to Henry Cornelius Agrippa, and from a plethora of earlier Hermetic, Dark Ages, Medieval, Renaissance, and later Transition Era magical tracts.

In fact, there is nothing new about the New Age at all, other than its fragmented, imbalanced attempts to eclectically synthesize the magic from these earlier sources into its own peculiar 'modern' system(s). It is because of this latter condition, coupled with the current absolute lack of Kabbalistic analysis of ritual and ceremonial performance, that this book was written.

Thus, this book, along with the others I have written, are a *reaction against* what is loosely called the New Age. This is a reaction not only against its ineffective attempt at eclectic synthesis, but a reaction against a further determination to weld that attempted synthesis into a type of syncretism: the action of combining diverse forms of religious and philosophical beliefs into a new quasi-religious system—a system that simply does not work.

The resulting theological pabulum, theosophical mishmash, and Kabbalistic abuse that fills the pages of so many "contemporary" books on the subject, provides the modus operandi behind this absolute failure. The practitioner may have already realized this—or will—after his or her diligent attempts to apply the tenets of these new systems that fall under the heading of New Age. The result? Personal magical failure, all around.

The oft abused Golden Dawn *system* of magic as it appears today in so many variations, is *the* example of failure I have in mind. Thus, because this book is a reaction against the New Age with material anything but new, I do not have to concern myself with creeping back into the mainstream of modern magic. Indeed, it is my opinion that there is no modern magic, except insomuch as Hermetic, Dark Ages, and Old System material has been edited, distorted, interpreted, re-interpreted, re-applied, re-reapplied, and twisted into new forms, all in an attempt to fit the contrivances of New Age dandies who fancy themselves magicians, by continually deluding themselves as to any results of their 'magical work.'

In effect, my disdain is not for the material the New Age claims as its own, but for its dilettante treatment of that material. If the reader will carefully reread this argument, he or she will quickly see my position could not therefore be otherwise.

This book will deal with the theoretical underpinnings—the foundational substance and theoretical substructure—which must be applied to any and all of the ritual and ceremonial performances of contemporary magical thought, before those rites will bear the fruit desired by the genuine aspirant to magic. Magic is not a personal convenience. Neither is it an intellectual contrivance nor a quick-fix for any of life's challenges. Magic is a Work that extends over years, decades, and yes, over lifetimes. It is the most grueling discipline ever conceived of, and devised by, humankind. Magic is a discipline that *eventually* results in an eclectically-balanced, **personal System of Magical Practice**, the individual elements of which *are the particular practices specific to each magician's own inner nature.*

Why do I so adamantly stress a *personal* system of magical practice? One size fits all does not apply here. That is why any cookbook approach to the subject is doomed to fail. No two individuals are the same in any way, much less the same as to their objective understanding of any given subject and the subjective methods in which they apply that understanding to their inner and outer conditions and circumstances. Hence the need for a carefully designed, carefully constructed state of personal, subconscious Subjective Synthesis. Unless the magician's mind is so trained, such that his or her subconscious (or unconscious, if you prefer) contains within it a structured, clear, well-connected understanding of the *theoretical principles* and *operational mechanisms* not only behind a specific magical action but also of its supporting theoretical substructure—the Kabbalah—the individual will end up receiving no results, partial results, or worst of all, negative results.

This process of developing one's subconscious magical structure, which I refer to as the individual's State of Subjective Synthesis and which has been thoroughly explained in my previous book on Ceremonial Magic, will be greatly aided by the practitioner's judicious use of this Handbook. This is a Handbook—literally a concise reference book—that is meant to be studied *closely*, and used *daily*.

By doing so, the individual practitioner of magic will not only integrate his or her existing knowledge of Kabbalah into an ordered subconscious whole, thereby achieving a dynamic state of Subjective Synthesis, but will have at the ready a wealth of those pertinent attributions, correspondences, theological principles, and sundry philosophical details that can very well turn empty ritual results into living, powerful achievements for the practicing magician.

But my readers should also be aware of something else that may be as great an aid to them in their practical magical work, as are the consequences of the study of the theoretical Kabbalistic material presented herein. While writing this book, I came to realize that a handbook for Kabbalah, as important as this may be, was actually insufficient in and of itself. Why?

Because it became glaringly apparent that due to the prevalence of the Golden Dawn current and its associated offshoots, this handbook would be of no use to the aspirant to magic if the information it provided was introduced in the same tired, patched together manner found in the seemingly unlimited presentations of present day Golden Dawn type material. That is, no matter how hard I tried to provide a unique, usable format, questions as to its use in ritual and ceremonial practices were still left wanting.

Thus, although I did not originally intend to do so, I finally came to the conclusion that I needed to add a course component to this handbook, to aid the practitioner to effectively *coordinate* the Kabbalistic information provided herein, with their practice of Golden Dawn type magical material. As I continued to write, I further realized that the course component would have to be an exposé of the unique system of Western Magic that I hammered out for myself over a period of three-plus decades, and which I have privately taught to a considerable number of others.

In effect, you the reader now possess not only a highly functional handbook of Kabbalah, but also a 'system' that will effectively instruct you in the proper practice of Golden Dawn type ritual and ceremonial acts. Use this book well. Make it your constant companion during the planning phases of your ritual and ceremonial work. I guarantee that if you do, you will bless the day you accepted this council.

Above all, use this book as you *continue to make a methodical study of the Kabbalah proper*, which is what you *must* do if you are serious about growing as a human being, *and* developing and balancing all of your magical abilities. That is, study the Kabbalah as it exists beyond the compendious form presented here. I have provided some references at the end of this book to help you in this study. Consider them well. While what is presented in this volume is not in cookbook style, of necessity, it is concise.

How can something be concise without exhibiting cookbook properties? Because it is meant for those who already have some knowledge of Kabbalah and are willing to acquire more, as well as for those who are willing to undertake this fascinating journey into Kabbalah, but do not know where to start. Make no mistake about it. Your mastery of the Kabbalah—that is, glimpsing its deepest philosophical aspects, comprehending its most beautiful doctrines, obtaining the vision of its host of spiritual insights, as well learning to apply it in its practical applications—is absolutely necessary if you are to succeed in your overall life's work.

In my opinion, your overall life's work should be one of growth, in the order of intellectual, emotional, psychic, material, and spiritual growth. If you follow this Path, sparing yourself no end of labor and toil, you will arrive. Nor will you will need to *depend* upon luck as you make the journey. For Luck is a fickle mistress as you have so often heard. But it is equally true that chance favors the prepared mind, and with your growing knowledge of Kabbalah and this handbook—designed to help you in both your theoretical investigations and their practical applications—you will find the opportunities Lady Luck presents to you will, in the main, work to your advantage.

Why do I say this? Because when you prepare your mind in advance through your tireless efforts of learning and applying the Kabbalah, the most sublime form of all philosophical wisdom, you will see matters in a new light. You will perceive yourself, others, and the tides of fortune differently. The fabric of your daily reality will actually undergo a transformation, as you come to understand and know the inner workings of issues and circumstances at levels which may be beyond your immediate consciousness, but are still accessible to your reasoning mind and intuitive faculties, just when you need them.

These are not promises. They are guarantees. They are not made by me to you, but by the Kabbalah itself, and these guarantees stand fast as they have throughout nearly two millennium, for all who undertake its methodical study, rigorous mental discipline, and daily practice. Do this and you will succeed in your life's work.

Foreword

Dr. Lisiewski and I first discussed the possibility of his writing this book in September of 2004. Having finished his second book, *Kabbalistic Cycles and the Mastery of Life,* he felt that he could legitimately expand the amount of material in that second book in several ways, and so the idea of *The Kabbalistic Handbook* came into being. Originally, I encouraged him to expand on the Kabbalistic principles given in the *Kabbalistic Cycles* book, and to add some additional details that might prove helpful to those readers who had little or no background whatsoever in the Occult, much less in Magic. Our discussions on the matter over the ensuing month or so provided more ideas, and so with my encouragement, he went to work on this third effort in November of last year.

But as so often happens with these things, the book took on a life of its own. As he wrote, he told me of the new direction the book was taking. "It's as if I have little to say about its contents" he complained. "It's just going in a direction I don't care to write in at this time." What he meant was that he was being prodded to put down on paper some of his most private and personal magical practices he had evolved over the course of his forty-odd years in Magic, and which he taught privately only to his personal students. What's more, those practices were completely in Western Magic—a "system" of Magic as he termed it in his other books— that he uses "...at odd times," always favoring the magic of the Medieval grimoires instead. "There are too many problems trying to make these Western magical practices come to life on paper" he told me. Nevertheless, he continued to write.

In February of 2005 he telephoned me and said, " I've been at it for four months now, and something is happening. I'm either going to have to scrap the book, or open myself up completely to this nagging, prodding influence that's driving me crazy, and put it all down so that it works as completely for the reader as it does for my private students and myself." I encouraged him to bite the bullet and do just that. Grudgingly he listened to my advice, and continued to write. (Sometimes I really have to get on Joe to get things done the way I *know* they should be done!) When I saw the final manuscript, I was very glad that I gave him the counsel I did, and that he followed it through. For my own four-plus decades of working, writing, and teaching in the field of magic were the only things that prepared me for what I found in this, his latest book.

Essentially, he gives the core theory and practice of Western Magic by focusing upon, and explaining in stark detail:

1. The importance of the magician's thoroughly knowing the symbolism underlying *any* ritual and ceremonial performance; and specifically, what this symbolism means in terms of that performance, and how it is used by the psyche in producing the results desired.

2. The absolute necessity of, and the method by which the student can establish his or her own eclectically balanced state of subconscious subjective synthesis—a rigorous and essential type of 'subconscious integrity and continuity' that is vitalized by the symbolic meaning of the magical symbols used in a give rite. He quite literally takes the reader 'by the hand' so to speak, and walks him or her through a step-by-step process he terms "Kabbalistic Analysis," in order to ensure the individual's subconscious super and substructures are well in place. In turn, these structures then assure that *any* ritual's performance will bear the fruit it is intended to produce.

3. A new and dramatic method by which the student of magic can use the Tarot cards as 'doorways' to—quite literally—enter into the energy *and identities* of the Paths of the Holy Tree of Life.

4. Another new method by which the student can then gain access to the Sephiroth themselves, after gaining entrance to the Paths.

5. After the magician has literally entered the Paths and Sephiroths, Joe then thoroughly reveals yet another technique by which the practitioner of magic can *consciously* and *willfully* direct the enormous power of the Paths and Sephiroth to achieve the practical, real-world, psychic, or 'spiritual' results he or she so sincerely desires.

6. A dialogue and elaboration—along with additional techniques—insisting that for magic to be authentic, it needs to demonstrate consistent and repeatable results, along with further methodologies by which this repeatability can be achieved.

If this isn't enough, Joe then continues on to give a coordinated approach to Western Magic by using not only the original Golden Dawn material, but augmenting it with several other well known texts. In this way, he provides the student of magic with what virtually amounts to a 'course' in the theory and practice of Western Magic, unlike any other I have seen to date. And from my own personal work in the fields of Magic and Occultism, I know that what he advocates in this book works.

I also want to caution the reader at this point. This is not a book that can be flipped through or casually used in a relaxed or irresponsible way. This is genuine 'meat' material; not "New Age" childish pabulum. It will require your careful, conscious attention to detail, a thorough understanding of its contents, and your full effort in working its principles ritualistically and ceremonially—just as is required by the nature and basis of all True Magic. Follow my words of advice here and you, the reader, will most definitely obtain the results you want from your magical work. It's as simple as that. 'Something for nothing' does not apply to any of Joe's books, much less to this one. So be prepared to *work*—and to *profit* most handsomely from that work!

But please be aware that if you take this work on, you will be very busy discovering your own powers and basic nature—which, for the majority of New Agers, is the last thing they wish to know. But there is little to worry about as the work required here is beyond even their imaginings and self-inflation.

— Christopher S. Hyatt, Ph.D.
South America, June, 2005

Chapter One

Concerning the Understanding and Use of this Book: A Guide to its Scope, Structured Format, Course Content, and Application

Scope of this Book

There are many fields of investigation and experimentation that fall under the general heading of Occultism: from general scrying to scrying in Spirit Vision; from Divination and its two most popular forms, the Tarot and the Pendulum, to the less used Geomantic Divination; from methods and techniques for developing the openly declared psychic functions of telepathy, concentration, clairaudience, clairvoyance, and telekinesis, to astral projection, mental projection, and mediumship; from magic in all of its broadband spectral majesty, to its specific practices of invocation and evocation, planetary and talismanic magic, Sephirotic and Path working investigations, to name but a few of the areas within the magical arts proper.

All of these occult-designated realms are, perhaps surprisingly, addressed by the Kabbalah. For instance, one may not see how the faculties of telekinesis and telepathy could be covered by Kabbalistic doctrine. Yet, in his intriguing and important book, *Sefer Yetzirah. The Book of Creation in Theory and Practice*, Rabbi Aryeh Kaplan insists that owing to the dynamic energy contained within the spiritual realm, the Sephirothic Worlds, the soul itself and the nature of angels, the *Sepher Yetzirah* is actually an "...instructional manual, describing certain meditative exercises...meant to strengthen the initiate's concentration, and were particularly helpful in the development of telekinetic and telepathic powers."[5]

If this is so—and in reality it most certainly is—then we are at once confronted with an overwhelming mass of Kabbalistic material from which we are somehow suppose to extract the essential tenets that apply to any given occult activity or investigation. Fortunately for us, we are only concerned here with that scope of the Kabbalistic framework that supports the most active realms of what is typically referred to as Western Magic.

Why should we differentiate so precisely only Western Magic? Because while the magical writings of the Dark Ages, the Medieval era and the later Renaissance and Transition Era periods are most certainly western in terms of the *dates* of those writings, the material of those writings originated with the earliest Egyptian Mystery religions, and was synthetically expanded into an intellectual Hermetic form by the ancient Western Greek civilization over a period of circa 330 B.C.E. to 400 C.E.

This *effective*, **workable** synthesis occurred to such a magnificent extent that its resulting theory and ritual framework is now thought by us to be western in composition, whereas in fact it is not. I mention this because it is important for one to keep the facts straight, and at the same time honor the roots of the magico-philosophical system known as Western Magic which is in such strong and universal use today.

At first glance it appears we can apply parts of the Kabbalah to *all* of the magic arbitrarily placed under the label of Western Magic. If this is so, we should be able to *immediately* apply it to the original source material as well, which is to say the magic of the grimoires of the Dark Ages, the Medieval period, and to the later Renaissance and Transition Eras. But this is not a correct assumption.

As I have argued on earlier occasions, this source material possesses very little in the way of Kabbalistic injunctions—at least, as it appears on the surface. The reason for this is that many of those Dark Ages, Medieval, and Renaissance grimoires contain extremely little text of *stated* Kabbalistic requirements, save for the days, hours, and seasons of magical operation. And in many cases, different grammars employ their own hourly and seasonal system.

Yet, with a knowledge of Kabbalah, the individual can quickly come to understand that Kabbalistic tenets *are* indeed either inferred or buried within some of the grammars, or else are implicit in the directions, which means implicit in the particular aspects of Kabbalah the author of the grimoire *expects* the individual to know by heart. Kabbalah *can* and *should* be applied to *all* parts of what we will soon define as Western Magic. But overall, the Dark Ages, Medieval, and Renaissance magical sources can safely be excluded, since those early forms of magic do not require such application in order for them to work as they were intended to.

Admittedly, this may be a difficult point to understand. Pausing to reread and carefully consider the above argument should assist in grasping the importance of this theoretical point. However, if the practitioner is adamant in applying a rigorous Kabbalistic treatment to those grimoires, it must be applied *only* after one's Kabbalistic foundation has been well laid, and the individual subjective synthesis superstructure has been firmly stabilized upon it.

Even so, I caution you. It is amazingly easy to imagine a nested, implied, or hidden Kabbalistic concept or principle in those grimoires, where there is none. Such self-induced misconceptions are perhaps the most dangerous of all when carried into actual practice, or worse yet, when they are integrated into one's own state of subjective synthesis. Once again, I strongly recommend the reader reread and meditate upon this discussion.

What then is Western Magic? What is its range? How do we apply Kabbalah to it every step of the way? And most importantly, *why* must we apply it? The answers to these seemingly innocuous questions are vitally important, for they will not only clarify the entire field of magical operations under which we can intelligently operate while in the Western System, but the answers will also automatically indicate the specific areas of Kabbalistic knowledge we must possess if we are to achieve the results we want our ritual and ceremonial performances to produce.

In effect, the answers to these simple questions will enable us to reduce the seemingly impossible task of mediating the depth and breadth knowledge of the vast scope of Kabbalistic literature into that which is strictly necessary to effectively work Western Magic, while remaining integrally sound enough to enter the practice safely and sanely.

Let us consider these questions one at a time. First, *what* am I defining as Western Magic? By Western Magic, I mean *that set of ritual and ceremonial performances that has been synthesized from Old System magical material, and which are currently and generally classed under the heading of Golden Dawn-type magic.* Notice that by this definition, I am not treating either the teachings of the original Golden Dawn material nor any of its current interpretations, off-shoots, schools, organizations, or systems of thought as artificial structures to be slavishly followed in a religious sense.

Rather, the definition provided will ironically enable the reader to find—if he or she has not already done so—that *individual* ritual and ceremonial performances taken from the original, eclectically imbalanced, unsound syncretic system material will indeed work *as they were intended to work,* but *only* after their Kabbalistic foundations are understood and applied in performance. In other words, these performances will *only* produce partial or incomplete results when operated as is. However, when the Kabbalistic insights are added to those ritual and practices, *complete results* are achieved.

As to the *range* of Western Magic, we find that the ritual and ceremonial performances comprising its practice can be loosely and very generally divided into the following nine categories:

- Preparatory magical practices
- Invocation and Evocation
- Planetary and Talismanic Magic
- Elemental Magic
- Zodiacal Magic
- Enochian Magic
- Sephirothic Magic
- Divinatory Magic
- Path Working Magic

How do we apply Kabbalah to the ritual or ceremonial actions of Western Magic as a whole, and to the component parts of those rituals? The answer to the 'how' lies in first considering another 'what.' For instance. What do the colors and actions of the Kabbalistic Cross mean from a Kabbalistic perspective when used to 'Open and Close the Temple Proper' as I refer to the preparatory ritual of the Lesser Banishing Ritual of the Pentagram?

While many students of Western Magic perform this simple composite ritual daily, few have ever bothered to consider the Kabbalistic meanings of the components of the ritual, or of the ritual as a whole. Yet it is this very Kabbalistic understanding that vivifies and vitalizes this composite ritual through the individual's state of subjective synthesis. Upon considering questions such as these, the 'how' now becomes apparent. That is, we *apply* this philosophical knowledge and understanding, and apply it in three ways.

The first way we apply this mystical knowledge is by obtaining a mediate breadth and depth of Kabbalistic knowledge, such as is presented in the chapters of this book. This knowledge acquisition will lay the foundation for the individual's state of subjective synthesis, or will strengthen their existing foundation if they already possess a sound knowledge of Kabbalah.

The second way is through the *conscious application* of this knowledge by analyzing each ritual and ceremonial practice in an effort to understand the Kabbalistic forces working behind and through both the individual parts of the practice, and the practice as a whole.

The third method of usage becomes automatic over time. As daily ritual work proceeds, the insights, inspirations, and intuitive gleanings derived through the conscious application of Kabbalah to that work, will, as the ritual and ceremonial practices continue over time, build up into a magical superstructure.

Although I have made every attempt to make this book as user friendly and as applicable as is possible to the different forms of Western Magic to be discussed in the next section of this chapter, it is up to the individual practitioner to *apply* it to the myriad number of rituals that exist within any of the categories of magic described earlier. That is, it is not possible for anyone to open this book to the section on Kabbalah, and find every attribute of every component of the dozens of rituals—whether composite or individual—and the thousands of variations that exist within them, *with the Kabbalah already applied.*

This is not a cookbook. Rather, it is a functioning sourcebook for the student. He or she must remain diligent and thoughtful in their analysis of each ritual and each of its component parts, if they are to derive the benefits and results they desire from their magical work. In short, no one can do the work for the individual.

This is a personal work, as different as is each individual's approach to it and understanding of it; as different for each individual, as are the number of unique people on this earth. Only in this way can one's work of building an individual state of subjective synthesis in Kabbalah result in what they desire most: reaping the personal rewards from their magical actions, and reaping those rewards as completely as possible.

Why must Kabbalah be rigorously applied to all Western Magical practice? For the very reasons stated above. *Kabbalah must be applied for the proper formation and strengthening of one's own state of subjective synthesis, which then acts as a channel through which the living forces of the Kabbalah can flow. For it is these vitalizing forces that breathe life into one's ritual and ceremonial performances, in addition to stimulating and activating the wellspring of psychic energy latent within the deepest strata of the magician's being, and through which the ritual and ceremonial performances manifest the desired result.* When this happens, the practicing magician attains what he or she most probably has not heretofore attained—complete and total results. Now the magical work bears the fruit it was intended to.

Structured Format of this Book

It may not seem too incredulous to many readers who have read this far, that most current day practitioners of the Art and Science of Magic do not use the Kabbalah to analyze their magical practices. Instead, they typically revert to some New Age book as is to 'work' their magic. In other words, these practitioners quite literally proceed to practice in a cookbook fashion. They probably have no intellectual understanding of what they are doing, why they are doing it, or the 'why of the how' behind their ritual movements, imaging, intonation of divine name, and all the rest of it. After all, that's what the New Age 'process' of 'Enlightenment' is all about, right?

The 'one size fits all' mentality prevails under its casual aegis. But what may astound many—perhaps even the present reader?—is that these same practitioners never so much as pause to even consider the category or branch of Western Magic they are 'practicing' from at any given time. They have no differentiated, fixed reference points within their minds—and therefore within their state of subjective synthesis—from which to work intelligently, purposely, and *willfully*.

In short, intellectual, philosophical, and theological harmonium is completely lacking in their magical world. Every partial, incomplete, and fragmented magical idea—and any Kabbalistic knowledge that they may possess—all run together, with the overlap causing no end of ritual difficulties in actual practice. In turn, daily life problems are experienced as a direct result of improperly performed rituals. The very idea of applying Kabbalah to a ritual or ceremonial performance as a composite act—let alone to its component parts—is completely missing from the mental states of most if not all New Age subscribers.

To acquaint readers with the effort that will be required of them, and in a modest attempt to support getting use to approaching the art aspect of magic in a scientific way, the concise categories of magic listed earlier have been expanded here. It is my intention that this simple expansion will aid the reader to first of all consider what area of magic they intend to work in, thus enabling them to focus on the specifics of that area. In turn, this differentiation will enable them to establish fixed reference points, allowing their states of subjective synthesis to develop fully and completely, so they can work intelligently, purposely, and willfully.

Preparatory magical practices — Those magical rituals such as Pentagram Rituals, Hexagram Rituals, Analysis of the Keyword, Rose Cross Rituals, Assumption of God forms and so on, that are preliminary to other magical work within a given ritual or ceremonial act, or which are used as ritual acts in and of themselves. That is, in the latter instance, these basic ritual actions can serve as self-contained, individual magical actions that are not a part of a larger magical effort.

An example of such a self-contained action would be the performance of the Lesser Banishing Ritual of the Pentagram as a daily cleansing, purification, and self-dedication rite. Of course, such a basic ritual act can be built up into a composite ritual. For instance, one can begin with the performance of the Kabbalistic Cross to 'Open,' followed by the Lesser Banishing Ritual of the Pentagram, and then 'Close' with another Kabbalistic Cross performance. From here, the magician can proceed with the Analysis of the Keyword to 'Open' once more, follow through with the performance of the Lesser Banishing Ritual of the Hexagram, and finally, conclude by 'Closing' the entire composite ritual action with another Analysis of the Keyword.

Invocation and Evocation — With Invocation, the magician calls down, or calls upon, Archangelic or Angelic beings, or beings who are traditionally designated as divine, or calls upon the innate part of God—the Yechidah—within the deepest recesses of his or her own nature, for the purpose of attaining 'spiritual enlightenment' (actually, psychic unfoldment), protection, power, or as an aid in some specific way to further one's own magical work or life experience. This form of magic can act as a preparation for other work to be done in the same composite ritual act or performance, or it can be a single self-contained act.

In Evocation, the magician is calling up or summoning forth the Infernals—which are those demons typically referred to as "The Fallen Angels"—to full physical manifestation, for the purpose of having them perform such acts or actions as are in keeping with the expressed Will of the magician (or Operator). Unless the magician is in full control of his or her psychic faculties and emotional nature, and can control the mind consciously, carefully, and logically, this most dangerous of all branches of magical work will inevitably end in tragedy of the worst kind for the practitioner.

Planetary and Talismanic Magic — Planetary magic involves invocation or calling down the forces ascribed to each of the Seven Planets of the Ancients: Saturn, Jupiter, Mars, the Sun, Venus, Mercury, and the Moon. Planetary Magic is accomplished through some composite ritual or ceremonial act, for the purpose of harnessing, directing, or communicating with those forces in order to fulfill some specific end as designed by the magician.

Talismanic Magic concerns itself with calling down planetary forces, as well as invoking other forces inherent in magically derived names, letters, and symbols, for the purpose of imbuing a device inscribed with those letters, symbols and so forth. Such a device will then be charged with those forces it is intended to represent. The talisman serves to either attract those desired objects, events, or conditions directly or indirectly from the environment of the magician, or to call forth talents, abilities, attitudes, or patterns of behaviors from within the psychic nature of the practitioner, or from the deeper subconscious strata or substrata of the magician.

Elemental Magic — A form of Western Magic that involves the invocation of the Angels and forces of the Enochian Tablets of the Elements for the purposes of achieving some mundane, psychic, or 'spiritual' purpose. While based on the tenets of Enochian Magic, in and of itself it is not Enochian Magic. Rather, it is a clever and astute application of Enochian principles in a unique framework.

It differs immeasurably from the grimoiric-type Elemental Magic of the Gothic Revival Era Magic (1800–1900 C.E.) as practiced, for instance, by Eliphas Levi. It is almost unrecognizable from the earlier goetia-based attempts of the Medieval Era (1000–1453 C.E.) and the Renaissance Era period (1460–1600 C.E). In my opinion, however, the 'new' Western form is preferable since it lends itself to more frequent practice. (This westernized invocation of the spirits of the Elements is covered splendidly in David Griffin's book, which will be cited formally in the Course Content section that follows.)

Zodiacal Magic — A synthetic form of Western Magic that invokes the forces of the Zodiac Signs. Due to the elemental correspondences of the Signs, the elemental forces of the Signs can be invoked through these practices. Additionally, there are procedures for stressing the planetary energy aspects of each sign, owing to the planetary attributions ascribed to each Sign also. Thus, Zodiacal, Elemental, or Planetary force aspects of the Signs can be invoked through properly performed zodiacal magical rituals.

Enochian Magic — As opposed to Elemental Magic, Enochian Magic—by my own timeline definition—is a Renaissance Era form of magic received from spirit entities, and developed by the Elizabethan scientist, magician, and scholar, Dr. John Dee and his protégé, Edward Kelly. For all intents and purposes I consider it to be a completely unique, self-contained system of magic. Owing to this, it will be treated as such throughout this book.

Sephirothic Magic — Sephirothic Magic is a derived form of Western Magic. While in some ways it is similar in structure and composition to Elemental Magic, it calls upon the forces of a given Sephirah as an aid to accomplish some predetermined purpose.

Divinatory Magic — This is an ancient form of magic, concerned with the use of various mechanical methods and devices designed throughout history, for determining the outcome of events that lie in the future. In its simplest form, the various methods produce 'yes' or 'no' answers to a specific query. Its most popularly developed Western magical forms, the Tarot and Geomancy, yield 'complete pictures' of the forces underlying the issue being divined, their evolution throughout the development of the matter, and a final answer which is interpreted as an outcome due to the forces both surrounding and inherent in the issue.

Although these two western forms of divination may seem complex, they can, however, be extremely accurate. The accuracy is not simply due to the external forces operating in the matter being queried, but also due to the psychological interplay of the querent's conscious and subconscious mind (his or her state of subjective synthesis in the latter case) which is brought to the matter, and how the individual's mind interacts with the information received from the divination.

Path Working Magic — Although the rudiments of this practice can actually be found or inferred from ancient manuscripts, I consider this type of magic to be a fairly recent, highly synthetic, yet workable and productive form of magic that involves the magician interacting with the influences of the thirty-two Paths of the Holy Tree of Life. Interaction can be through meditation, concentration, or some ritual performance designed to bring about a state of resonance with the Path energy being invoked. In the final analysis, it is an extremely important branch of Western Magic from a practical and Kabbalistic point of view. However, it is subject to the deceits of the individual's ego to an exceedingly high degree, owing to the 'soft' methods of invoking and interacting with the forces so contacted.

Since I am trying to make this handbook—or sourcebook if you will—as self-contained as possible, the brief explanations above should help the reader to not only realize how necessary it is to recognize the branch of magic being practiced at any given time, but to impress upon him or her the necessity of being consciously aware of the need to categorize practices in the first place.

A small step in building up one's state of subjective synthesis? Of course. Necessary? I feel it is as necessary as are the more nebulous actions of ritual and ceremonial Kabbalistic Analysis, and the study of the larger Kabbalah proper for expanding and stabilizing one's subjective state. (As the reader may have guessed by now, each of my books contain information that is repeated in a liberal but careful manner so that by the very action of reading them and thinking the material over in a thoughtful or meditative way, the reader will be well on their way to enlarging, fine-tuning, and ordering their subjective world immediately. It is my way of assuring that their magic *does* indeed work, and works as soon as is reasonably possible.)

As to the overall structure of this book. The Kabbalistic correspondences, attributions, and associations that are provided in this book, will cover eight of the nine categories of magic listed above. The ninth category or branch of Western Magic that will not be addressed is that of Enochian Magic, owing to the fact that this Renaissance Era form of magic is an entirely separate branch of magic in and of itself.

The serious reader may wonder if Enochian Magic contains its own Kabbalistic attributions and correspondences. Of course it does. There is *nothing* (note well) to which Kabbalah does not apply, or *cannot* be applied. Your next thought may be whether these Kabbalistic attributions and insights are important? The short answer is most certainly. A more thorough explanation is that while the Kabbalistic insights and attributions are most certainly important, my experience is that this form of magic is so self-contained in and of itself that it must be mastered *as is* as much as possible before further Kabbalistic investigations into its structure, meaning, and practice can be undertaken.

As with any experimental work in new or frontier science, it is best to repeat the reported experimental designs *exactly* as published, *before* attempting to modify or change the existing variables of those original experimental procedures. Since this form of magic should not be investigated and analyzed until this prerequisite has been strictly fulfilled, it cannot be addressed in a book such as this. In the end—as with building up one's state of subjective synthesis—the study of the Enochian is an intensely personal effort, the inroads to which will be determined by one's own (by then) well structured, stable, state of subjective synthesis.

As I indicated earlier, if the individual is to attain a mediate breadth and depth of Kabbalistic knowledge that will allow effective work in any of the branches of Western Magic listed, as soon as is reasonably possible and without New Age instant gratification and quick-fix attitudes and tendencies entering into the efforts, then groundwork must be provided here. In a book such as this, which aspires to be both a usable handbook and functional sourcebook, it is imperative that the Kabbalistic knowledge be as complete as possible.

Such a presentation has been provided in Chapter Four, *Concerning the Kabbalistic Knowledge Necessary for Effective Magical Practice.* Study it well. Learn its contents. Contemplate what is given therein. Burn it into your memory. Meditate upon those philosophical concepts and theological ruminations until you understand them intuitively, intellectually, and magically, and then *continue* to reflect upon them until you *apprehend* them. That is, continue to study them until you understand them in such an intuitive and natural way, that they become a living part of your mind and psyche.

This will happen if you persist, and when it does—each time it does as different parts of the material are assimilated by you—it will be as if a small electric shock has been delivered to your body and mind. A powerful nervous current will course through you, causing you to feel as if you are wavering or losing your balance. It is an inner sensation that at first may be frightening. When this happens, you will *know* beyond all doubt that you have truly apprehended the material, and it has become a living, vibrant part of your nature, as intimate and personal to you as are your deepest, innermost private thoughts and feelings. Thus your subjective synthesis will proceed to be formed and stabilized, granting you the Key by which you can open the door to successful magical practice: a practice more powerful than your wildest dreams at this moment.

But the education of the reader in these salient magical matters goes further than this. Instructions will be provided on what I term *The Agrippa System of Planetary Hours of the Day and Night.* The student of magic will need to clearly understand this system and be able to work it accurately. Should the practitioner choose to employ it, this system of hours of the day and night will be found to provide the most reliable magical blueprint of all, enabling the magician to determine the best times to perform their daily ritual work.

If the reader begins to employ this system in their daily ritual and ceremonial work, I am quite certain they will elect to continue it as opposed to employing some New Age contrivance or as opposed to not using it at all. Although bare bones explanations of this system have appeared in print many, many times before, to the best of my knowledge, they have not been presented in an exact, complete, and thorough way, such that the student can work the system confidently on a daily basis. Again. Since this book is intended to be both a handbook and sourcebook, these instructions have been painstakingly provided in Chapter Three, *The Agrippa System of Planetary Hours of the Day and Night*.

In Chapter Four, Classical Kabbalistic material will be presented, which is the essence of this book. This material has been a part of the literature for at least the past four hundred years. New Age hodgepodge has been scrupulously avoided. The information presented is for the working magician, and as such, it may be viewed by many simply as hard data. Nevertheless, it is data relevant to whatever particular branch of magic the practitioner is working in at any given time, after they have identified the appropriate category.

It may be simply called hard data, but it is data that will save you hours to weeks of time, gathering such information on your own. Now you can go directly to the work at hand, which is changing your life through the application of magic. To repeat once more. You will have to apply this hard data to your practices yourself. No one can do that for you, owing to the vast number of ritual possibilities and perceptual variations that exist within any of the eight categories of magic to be examined.

Application of the Kabbalistic information is achieved through a concise analysis of each ritual and ceremonial performance: both of the component parts of a complete or composite ritual, as well as to the whole rite itself. Is this a lot of work? Absolutely! But all you have to ask yourself is whether you want *full* results and in *your* own way? Or do you want to 'kind of' work magic, only dreaming of full results because doing otherwise would be too much hard work? The choice is yours, and so will be the results. Therefore, choose wisely.

Originally, I intended to give a separate chapter for each of the eight categories of magic listed earlier. Granted, much of the same information would appear in each chapter, owing to the enormous number of ritual possibilities, the inevitable alterations the practitioner will weave into them, the different perceptual variations through which a given ritual can be viewed, as well as the commonality of much of Kabbalistic theory.

Thus, for example, a significant amount of Kabbalistic material that would have been presented in the chapter on Planetary and Talismanic Magic would also be found in the chapter on Preparatory Magic; and much of the information given in the chapter on Invocation and Evocation, would likewise have appeared in the chapter on Sephirothic Magic. In the end, such a format could not be justified beyond a ploy to lengthen the book, which would do the practitioner no good at all.

My first consideration is to write and structure this volume so it is easy to use, while remaining as complete in content as possible for application into immediate magical practice. Turning it into a strained, repetitive one would have resulted in a book that is either awkward to use, or else unusable. The final design is simple. A broadband set of Kabbalistic theology, theory, attributions, correspondences—both spiritual as well as material—will be presented in the chapters dealing with the Kabbalah. However, what should make all the difference to the practicing magician (as opposed to other magical literature) are the "Preliminary Remarks" in each of those chapters, along with the Kabbalistic data specifically culled for Kabbalistic analysis and ritual use.

This structure should allow four very important activities to take place:

- First, it provides the immediate Kabbalistic knowledge needed for the current magical work in which one is engaged.
- Second, by the sheer process of referring to the material while moving through different branches of magic, repetition of the material will almost automatically burn itself into the practitioner's memory and subconscious mind, thus enhancing and strengthening their state of subjective synthesis.
- Third, many of the component parts of a composite rite are indeed the same from category to category. For instance. The Lesser Banishing Ritual of the Pentagram (LBRP) can be performed as a simple, self-contained Prefatory Ritual, or as a component part of the consecration of a talisman. The magician will need to refer to sections on the proper-

ties of the corresponding Sephirah and the correspondences and attributions of the planet assigned to that Sphere for his or her initial Kabbalistic Analysis of the LBRP, and also the planetary considerations of ritual consecration itself. Certainly it is more desirable to have everything needed for any given phase of the work in one, single chapter, than to have to leaf back and forth through an entire book looking for the needed information.

- Fourth, such referencing technique not only allows the practicing magician to understand the interconnectivity that exists between the categories of magic, but it also enables one to grasp the theoretical substructure upon which this interconnectivity—and *all* of Western Magic for that matter—is so firmly based, which is the Kabbalah.

Since you now have some idea of the format and purpose of this book, let's proceed deeper into its structure and content.

Course Content

Now we know that it is necessary to ask what branch or category of Western Magic is being practiced, and also where it falls in the Western magical scheme. We understand the reasons for determining these things and can answer these questions precisely. Your next thoughts might follow thusly:

1. I realize that the statements made by this author about the Golden Dawn material as a system is only his opinion. However, for the time being I will assume he is right because up until now, I have not received the promised results from my Western magical work.

2. I also know that the contemporary expression of Western Magic is primarily through the system of the Golden Dawn, or some variation thereof. If, as a system, the Golden Dawn material is eclectically imbalanced and as a *whole* is syncretically unworkable, then that could explain my lack of results, no matter how diligent I've been and how hard I tried to make this system work throughout these many years.

3. So for the sake of argument I'll accept his position—but again, only just for the moment. My questions are:

A. How do I now go about practicing Western Magic effectively?
B. What books do I work from now, if indeed, the Golden Dawn material—as a magical *system*—is as frustrating to use as he says it is and indeed, as I have found it to be?

Only a kindergarten mentality would think that it could learn and practice all there is of any subject—much less Western Magic—from a single source. Yet, this is all too often the case when it comes to those who would practice this form of 'modern' magic. This self-generated delusional expectation generally stems from the individual's inability to handle life's challenges. The fear of consequences due to this inadequacy, then quickly becomes coupled to the deep-seated doubt they have of their own mental and psychic capabilities.

A powerful miasmatic mental and emotional condition then flows naturally from these internal states of chaos. These negative self-appraisals produce a panicked need to have or to make some 'one thing' work; one thing that will ease the pain of daily life. Should that 'one thing' fail to work for them as intended, their mental capacity to cope becomes frozen by their inability to handle complex life issues, and the fear that arises from that inability. The idea of having to resort to more than one system or to more than one book at a time—or even to compare material from one reference source with another—usually pushes such individuals completely over the psychological edge.

These neurotic dynamics thus operate powerfully in the subconscious realm—as well as in the conscious dimensions of the individual—preventing him or her from straightening out their lives through magic. They become damned, not *in* but *through* their limited study and restricted practice of magic, regardless of the era that magic is taken from, let alone in the overwhelmingly complex system generically known as Golden Dawn magic.

It is no different than wanting to undertake the study of, say, the Calculus. He or she would most probably go to their local university, sign up for the course, get the syllabus, buy the textbook, and—at first—might expect that single textbook to be the beginning and end of all the information they will ever need in order to *understand* and *effectively apply* the Calculus to the problems they have in mind. It is also true that in many such cases, the individual's self-doubts of their mathematical abilities might bring on a fear of failure of being able to learn the material in the first place, much less be able to apply this new material effectively.

But by and large, after some work, the student begins to grasp this point on the meaning of the limit and that idea behind Rolle's Theorem. Soon their confidence increases, and they begin to see that the Calculus is no different from any other area in which they initially lacked proficiency. They begin to understand that it takes time, study, and hard work to break though. But once they do break through, their self-confidence begins to soar, and they commence to question not only their Professor, but the textbook itself. Do the instructor's lectures correspond with the text, or is he using his own notes, expecting them to use the textbook to fill in? Does the text author write clearly, or is the author more interested in impressing fledgling students of the subject with his or her exalted knowledge of the secrets behind the Calculus?

Sooner than later, in many cases, the new student is off on their own voyage of mathematical self-discovery, talking to other professors or tutoring assistants, looking for other textbooks, problem and solution manuals and math dictionaries that are written in an *order and form* he or she can *understand* and *use*. In other words, the student is now developing his or her *own functional eclectic system* by which to *learn and use* the Calculus. While the subject material of the Calculus remains fixed as a *system of topics*, the individual's *approach* to those topics—and consequently their understanding of them—has become *harmoniously* eclectic in the truest sense of the word.

*In point of fact, as the student is achieving his or her goal, they are doing it by developing their own state of subjective synthesis in the subject. For an **effective** eclectic system in any subject is not simply limited to understanding and using the **content** of the subject, but also includes **the method of approach or order** through which the material makes sense, and therefore, 'works' for the individual. **In conclusion, an ordered state of subjective synthesis is the result of—not the cause behind—the approach used to build up one's personal eclectic system of thought and the eclectic system itself.** The* reader is advised to carefully restudy this example, for much is revealed in it.

After some further lengthy and intense struggle, adjustment and readjustment, that self-same student who was so incredibly doubtful of his or her mathematical abilities and frightened at the very prospect of this so-called intimidating subject, more often than not ends up helping fellow classmates who have not made these discoveries for themselves.

It is the same with the study and effective practice of Western Magic. The reader may already have studied the 'recommended' course textbook of the Golden Dawn material in one version or another, and in the 'classical order' recommended, and may even have had an instructor of sorts. But his or her initial and continued confusion over the *content, structure and order of presentation of that material as a system*, and how its teachings fit in with their own *personal perceptions*, have more often than not continued to conflict to the nth degree, instilling into the well-meaning aspirant a deep fear of failure.

This fear may have prevented them from beginning their own process of self-discovery of how those magical principles and practices are to be used by them, *and in the order that 'makes sense' to them*, in an *individual* way so that they can understand and effectively practice the material that constitutes the Golden Dawn source work. As a result, they have been left wanting for the results they need or desire, as they slavishly continue to 'work the *system*' as is. All to no avail.

So now it's time to look beyond the recommended textbook, and beyond that instructor you may have had, and get the wherewithal to get the job done, and get it done *right*.

It has been well known that Israel Regardie was my first mentor in magic, and later my very dear friend, from 1971 until his death in 1985. He initiated me into the Golden Dawn system in October of 1973 at his home in Studio City, California. During that time, Regardie and I had innumerable conversations concerning the GD as we referred to it. I have never admitted this before, but it seems right to do so now. To be honest, I took this initiation from Regardie *only* because of my admiration for him.

I was twenty-four years old at the time, but my heart was simply not in Western Magic. I had been practicing it for eight years. My argument with him was that I only received the results I wanted from my magical practices, by practicing what I even then referred to as the Old System of Magic, or that which is commonly known as the magic of the Dark Ages, Medieval, Renaissance, and Transition eras. Yet I continued to involve myself in this dual practice—both GD practices *and* my Old System work in Evocation to Physical Manifestation—for another twenty-three years, from 1973 through 1996. From 1996 onward, I concentrated upon Old System Magic exclusively, and still do today, for personal reasons.

At this point I must digress, but I trust this will benefit the reader in a number of ways. There were many times Regardie himself expressed to me his extreme displeasure with the GD as it is, and of its inability to produce the results it is supposed to. One evening, in 1978, after thirteen years of GD practice, and following a lengthy conversation with Regardie, I found myself blurting out to him, "Francis, I can't help it! I'm of the Old System, and always will be!" The words no sooner left my mouth when I realized that I must have insulted him very badly, and I was very frightened of the wrath I was certain to incur from him.

To my absolute astonishment, he looked at me—almost grimly but with a strange, wry smile—and replied, "Frankly, Joe, so am I!" To those readers who are upset by these statements, so be it. I *cannot* and *would not* change them if I could. Facts are facts, and this is factual. But Regardie was absolutely mesmerized by the beauty and grandeur of the initiatory rituals of the GD and so, *maintained his allegiance to that material as a system unto itself*, even though he knew its incredible shortcomings. To the contrary, I was not at all either spellbound or particularly interested in what I considered to be, and still do even more so, the Victorian stylistic, Freemason-like pomp and pageantry that masquerades beneath the GD ritualistic initiations.

It is my opinion, derived from my personal experience over the decades—and the practitioner may also come to realize this if they have not already—there is only One who can confer True Initiation. That Being is ever beside the individual and at their deepest center at all times. The Holy Guardian Angel (HGA) and the individual are inseparable. It is to this Being that all preliminary magical effort and work is to be dedicated, all with absolute purity of heart and motive, so that the True Initiation can eventually be conferred by this divine being.

The True Initiation can come at a moment's notice, either during or after a ritual or ceremonial performance, or at a least expected time. It can come in steps of interior illumination, culminating with what I call The Visitation. As I have found out, these latter processes are quite common for the magician who attempts to Attain to the Knowledge and Conversation of the Holy Guardian Angel (Attain to the K&C of the HGA) by the synthetic rituals of Western Magic, as opposed to performing the Abramelin Operation in its classic entirety.

Nevertheless, it *does* occur though the use of Western techniques, and in any of the ways noted above. As I see it, the pomp, the pageantry, the masquerading of manmade and directed initiations are all vainglorious events, meant to placate and exalt the weakest of egos—both of the initiators and the one being initiated. In my estimation, they are as "...such things are for fools, who lack the sense of cows..." as Crowley so well stated in his poem, "Jean," referring to matters that could most certainly include this issue. The reader need only study the history, personalities, and disintegration of the original Order of the Golden Dawn in 1900—and the fate of so many groups that sprang from it throughout the twentieth century—to understand *some* of the reasons I hold to this view.

As for me, having been a member and later the Chancellor of an Argentum Astrum magical organization from the mid-1970s through the early 1980s, and then a member of one of the Temples of the Golden Dawn here in the United States from the mid-1980s to the early 1990s, I found from experience all I needed to know about the virtues of such membership. To this day I practice alone.

But this is only my experience. It is left to the intelligent reader to decide for themselves if membership in some magical group or another is or is not warranted, and to derive from such a decision the experiences attendant thereto. In the end, it may be that the hard-working reader will find as I have found that the expediencies of magical order initiation—relished as an *absolute mandatory* requirement, and demanded as such beyond all else by so many students and initiators alike—are only held high by those who are either incapable or unwilling to *work* for the moment when Godhead makes its Holy descent into Manhood of Its Own volition: *the* ultimate reward for the magician's absolute dedication and hard work.

I have given an account of these matters here as they may have bearing upon the reader's understanding of many things that can occur at different points in one's magical career. But additionally, I have included this discussion as a prelude to an explanation of the Course material that is to follow.

What then can the desirous student do to effectively involve themselves in this so called Golden Dawn current of Western Magic? And of equal importance, *how* can this era-type magic be used to produce the full results the practitioner is so desperately seeking? Without further extensive elaboration of that which must logically follow from all that has been written up to this point, suffice it to say that I have found Western Magic to be extremely effective when the following books are used *in tandem* to work the *material*—not the *system!*—of the Golden Dawn, which will be explained.

In the first instance, the answer to 'what' the individual can do to effectively practice Western Magic so as to yield the results it is intended to yield—be they spiritual (actually, psychic), mental, emotional, or material—is to use the following sources, in the manner recommended here. In my four-plus decades of magical practice in general, and thirty-one years of work with the GD material in particular, I have found this 'coursework' to be extremely efficient. It has proven to be efficient for myself and for the many students I taught privately throughout the years, *after* their state of subjective synthesis was first attended to. These resources are:

• *Three Books of Occult Philosophy*[3]—Ascribed to Henry Cornelius Agrippa of Nettesheim, these books are literally what they are advertised to be: the foundation books of Western Occultism. They constitute, again as advertised, a virtual doctoral degree in Magic. Written in the early part of the sixteenth century, this magnum opus acts as a lens, directing the many and varied rays of Dark Ages and Medieval era magic, and projecting those rays through the Renaissance and other magical eras that followed, finally bringing those ray-like projections to a focal point in what we term the Western Magic of today. They are the single most important research and reference resources that the practitioner of any era of Magic—be it Dark Ages, Medieval, Renaissance, Transition, Postmodern, Western, or anything in between—can own.

• *The Complete Golden Dawn System of Magic*[6]—Why this tome if it is ineffective as a system? The answer is the exact reciprocal of the question: the reader is not trying to mimic, implement, or imitate that confused, ineffectively patched-together eclectic structure as a *unified system* with the eventual idea of worshipping it in a syncretic way as their substitute religion. Rather, *The Complete Golden Dawn System of Magic* should be utilized as a *framework* for building one's state of subjective synthesis *in terms of* the Knowledge Lectures it contains, and for familiarizing oneself with the original Order ritual and ceremonial performances, philosophical ideas and so on, that make up this system.

This is extremely important in order to establish a reference baseline, that is, a fixed reference point against which ritual and ceremonial details and actions—along with general occult and magical knowledge—can be weighed and measured in an analytical sense. Remember the example of the individual trying to learn Calculus? In the same way, after this outline of occult knowledge is attained, the student will gradually become confident, and strike out on his or her own journey of magical self-discovery. They can develop their own unique, *harmonious* eclectic system of magical practices, *and their approach to, or order of those practices,* that work for them efficiently, effectively, and with a natural regularity.

Then they will discover other magical textbooks that fill their own bill of understanding, comprehension and apprehension, as well as those that cater to their own developing, unique style of ritual and ceremonial technique. In short, this book, *The Complete Golden Dawn System of Magic*, serves to give the magician an *important outline—but an outline **only**—*of the knowledge necessary to work effectively in Western Magic.

Of course, the reader can very safely leave the confused initiations in it for that crowd of magical ne'er-do-wells who adamantly insist they 'need' these contrivances for their 'spiritual growth' or worse yet, must have them in order to do their 'magical work.' As I have said, when True Initiation is conferred upon the earnest, diligent aspirant, it will come from the One above: not from some magical group or society of psychologically imbalanced, smug, pseudo-intellectual pop-in-jays, who strut about displaying their Grades of the Order, and then go on to play at magic.

Be aware also, that there are several different publishers of the original Golden Dawn material, each one having produced a revised and enlarged edition of the original work. This being the case, I suggest that the reader acquaint him or herself with at least two different publisher's versions in order to obtain a more comprehensive view of that information. While the prototype Golden Dawn material—at least as presented in the original 1937–1940 four volume set—is a patched together effort, the system presented in these latter, different versions, makes it even more so due to restructuring, additions, changes, and the like that have been incorporated.

Thus, it is best the reader be aware of the variations that have been written into the original material by making the comparisons as suggested. LEARN TO THINK FOR YOURSELF! Additionally, please be aware that owing to these variations, the Kabbalistic Analysis of the Lesser Banishing Ritual of the Pentagram that appears here later on, will be a *proximal* version—a weighted average so to speak—mirroring the variations the reader would find in that ritual in the various versions of the Golden Dawn books.

• *The Ritual Magic Manual. A Complete Course in Practical Magic.*[7]—In the study of advanced mathematics, there are two approaches in presentation. As an illustration, in the Calculus, there are two independent ways of presenting both the theory and application of that material: the applied approach and the rigorous approach. While there isn't a Calculus textbook on the market today that doesn't make the claim that it presents a healthy balance of both approaches, the fact is that balance has never been struck in any of them. Indeed, when such attempts are made, the result is a confused distortion that causes new or even experienced students no end of agony. This probably sounds familiar to you because this is what you have no doubt found in those dozens, if not hundreds of books on Western Magic that fill your bookcases, and which never quite worked the way they promised to. The fact is, *differentiation of approach* is not simply helpful to learning, comprehending, and eventually apprehending any material. It is *absolutely necessary* in the presentation of new as well as advanced material in any field of study.

The solution to this differentiation in approach—which the practitioner will gradually *integrate* into his or her own eclectic, *personal system* of knowledge and magical practice—can be found in the careful use of this book, when used in tandem with *The Complete Golden Dawn System of Magic*. The author of *The Ritual*

Magic Manual, David Griffin (whom I do not know personally, and with whom I have never had any contact), has done what I consider to be the near impossible.

He has provided an applied approach to the structure, design, and application of Western Magic as defined by original source work, and in my opinion, has done so in the truest sense of the Kabbalistic ideal. Let me restate this more specifically so there can be no room for misunderstanding or misinterpretation. This author has not only produced Kabbalistically-correct and extremely detailed instructions for performing Golden Dawn-type magic—the applied approach—but has in the process produced a blended, rigorous presentation of it as well. (Let the authors of Calculus books out there listen and learn from him. It *can* be done!)

The Complete Golden Dawn System of Magic and other published versions of this material can thus be thought of as providing a pure, rigorous approach in that it only gives an *outline* of the subject matter. It does this in such a way however, by *presuming* the student either knows how to fill in the blanks, or else has access to other Order documents that will enable them to do so. It is this assumption that is one of the features that makes the treatment of *any* subject rigorous by strict definition. And this most certainly applies to *The Complete Golden Dawn System of Magic* as well.

In fact, as Regardie told me many times, this was the one assumption that he did not like. When the original Golden Dawn Order papers were prepared, it was known that the students of the original London-based Golden Dawn Temple of the late 1880s through early 1900s, were able to access the Order archives and fill in the material provided in the original Order document outlines. However, provisions were not made for others based at temples that were planned, and for those that could not access the archives for one reason or another.

As a result, this oversight or designed condition carried over to the Order writings as we know them today. By contrast, Mr. Griffin's text can be viewed as being an actual, effective, mathematically precise *integration* of both the applied and rigorous approaches that result in a stable, workable, highly-detailed, ordered whole, because he provided *missing ritual details and Kabbalistic treatment* of the Order work in some cases, while in other cases, he offers lines of thought that will point the way to filling in the blanks.

But it goes even further than this. Studying his ritual and ceremonial details, I have come to feel that he has applied the Kabbalah to this material in such an insightful way, that it will be a kind of automatic help to the student to further his or her *conscious* Kabbalistic Analysis of the rituals, which is *absolutely necessary* for building, ordering, and polishing one's own state of subjective synthesis.

And happily, there is even more in this very interesting compendium of magical practice. Mr. Griffin has expanded or intelligently synthesized a number of the branches or categories of magic cited earlier in a unique and powerful way, with his treatment of Elemental and Sephirothic Magic being just two such examples. I use the word powerful to mean just that, simply because my own lengthy involvement in Western Magic has forced me to derive many of the exact same ritual structures, interpretations and considerations myself, that he presents in his volume. Consequently, I know from experience that his ritual synthesis, structures and expansions, are indeed quite effective.

It will not take the hard working student of Western Magic much time to realize the value of this book, *The Ritual Magic Manual*, once he or she has begun to analyze their own ritual and ceremonial performances in the way I recommend here. Finally, Cris Monnastre (another individual with whom I have never had any contact), has provided an interesting, lucid, and concise Foreword to this book. It serves as an insightful inclusion which should also prove be of considerable value to the student.

• *A Kabbalistic Handbook for the Practicing Magician*. This handbook is important for its lucid instructions in the development of one's own personal, *balanced*, eclectic system of Western Magic, its content on Kabbalah, the application of the key concepts of Kabbalah as they are applied to the practice of Western Magic, as well as for the unifying effect it provides in these matters, thus providing a cohesive whole in terms of magical structure, theory, application, and practice. Additionally, it will go far in aiding the student to build up and order his or her own state of subjective synthesis.

Make no mistake about it. Other books will appear on the practitioner's intellectual horizons as their state of subjective synthesis develops and expands, and the individual becomes skilled in separating the wheat from the chaff. Remember. *Your task in your overall magical development, is to design and perfect your own, personal eclectic system of magic that works for you, and produces the results you want.* As I have said earlier, 'one size fits all' does *not* apply in the Realm of Magic. It never has, despite the trite, pop nonsense the New Age has foisted upon many a sincere student of the Mysteries, and it never will.

Once again, by developing this personal eclectic system of working magic, you will develop your state of subjective synthesis to a high degree of symmetry. In mathematics, symmetry is a condition that allows the image of a curve to look the same after it has been rotated about a given axis. In magic, symmetry occurs when your subconscious knowledge structure of the Kabbalah and the forces underlying each ritual and ceremonial performance (the rotation), works in harmony with magical forces invoked or evoked, and with your own subjective nature to such an extent, that regardless of the rituals or ceremonies you perform (the axis of rotation), your results will always look the same to you. In other words, you will produce the full results you desire, each and every time, variations in each performance (the image) notwithstanding.

Course Application

In the Course Content discussion, I began by saying, **what** can the desirous student do to effectively involve him or herself in this so-called Golden Dawn current of Western Magic? And of equal importance, **how** can this era-type of magic be used to produce the full results the practitioner is so desperately seeking? The 'what' has been answered in the previous discussion by recommending four books I have found that yield the practical results of Western magical work the practitioner either needs or wants to manifest in his or her life. But what about the 'how'? That is, *how* can these four books be used together, and worked from intelligently, so as to produce the required results? As the reader will see in the next chapter, nothing could be simpler.

Chapter Two

Concerning the Process of Kabbalistic Analysis

Preliminary Comments

Since most of us find it easiest to learn by example, a simple illustration should make the process clear in *how* to use these four books to 'make straight the way' in achieving understanding, comprehension, and apprehension of the principles of the Kabbalah. In doing so, this will eventually enable the magician to produce a personal, effective, eclectic system of ritual and ceremonial practice that will work for him or her with an astonishing regularity.

Let us take our example from that [deceptively] simple preparatory ritual, the Lesser Banishing Ritual of the Pentagram, which I have a habit of abbreviating in my personal magical journals as simply the LBRP. I am confining the example to this elementary, well-known ritual in order to convey three very specific points to the reader:

• Point One—Although the LBRP can function as a separate ritual act, it is actually composed of several components that really make it a basic composite ritual. By suggesting key questions in the analysis, this procedure will allow the reader to understand how the process of Kabbalistic Analysis can be used on both the component parts of a ritual, as well as on the resulting composite whole of a ritual or ceremonial act:

• Point Two—As the reader will soon see, this 'elementary' ritual, composed of only a few components, will mushroom as we begin to take it apart (analyze it) Kabbalistically, which is to say as we ask Kabbalah-based questions about it. As with trees of different sizes, the larger the tree, the more branches and limbs it can have, making it that much more beautiful and complex. The same is true with Kabbalistic Analysis. The more complex the ritual or ceremonial act, the more tree-like and therefore complex the analysis becomes. Yet without this analysis, the rewards of magic are few and paltry at best. Therefore, this simple example should serve to illustrate how the analysis is generally conducted, and should also answer questions about the mechanics of performing the analysis as well.

• Point Three—Doing such a simple analysis will lend the practitioner an insight into an amazing fact, one that is not easily explained, and which is even harder to understand. Nevertheless, it is a phenomenon whose understanding is both integral and crucial to the successful working of all magic. *No two individuals' states of subjective synthesis will be exactly the same, and yet each will produce the magical results intended.* By this I mean, that due to the mental matrix, personality structure, character base, and subconscious mental arrangement of each individual, no two Kabbalistic analyses will be based upon the same questions, proceed along the same lines, or be integrated into the subconscious strata in exactly the same way.

This will lead to different views, interpretations, and eventually, different understandings of both the Kabbalah, and how it and the Kabbalistic analysis applies to any and every ritual and ceremonial performance. *Thus, two different states of subjective synthesis will arise for any two practicing magicians. Yet, both will not only produce successful results, but highly similar or even the same results from the same ritual or ceremonial actions.*

The real world necessity and functional aspects of building and strengthening one's own state of subjective synthesis—*the* crucial requirement for each individual in order for his or her magic to work—thus becomes glaringly apparent. The 'why' of this phenomenon cannot be explained here, owing to the breadth and depth of psychoanalytical background the reader may or may not possess. In reality however, the acquisition of an *extensive* background in psychoanalysis—while touted from the highest pinnacles of nearly every Western magical group, society, and organization as being absolutely necessary for one's 'understanding' of Western Magic—*is neither necessary nor, in most cases, desirable for the magician to acquire in order for his or her magic to work successfully.*

Why is this so? Because as even the most rudimentary study of psychoanalytical literature will abundantly demonstrate, for any given psychological event or condition, there are a myriad number of schools of thought offered to explain it. In the end, after decades of diligent study, the magician will be left with a hodge-podge of intellectual misconceptions that are neither clearly integrated into his or her conscious understanding, nor properly placed into the subconscious state of subjective synthesis. Such is the highly inductive, uncertain nature of the field of psychoanalysis.

However, in those cases where such an integration is skillfully and correctly achieved, the student will inevitably find that he or she favors one school of psychoanalytical thought over the others. At first, this is fine, as it will suffice to provide the practitioner with intellectual insights into magical work—for a time. But as the magic becomes more complex, the school of psychoanalytical thought adopted will begin to break down, and it will be unable to answer both the 'why' as well as the 'how' of the 'why' of those complex ritual and ceremonial performances.

In the end, the mass of psychoanalytical literature that the magician has labored over for decades to understand, will be found to be no more than an interesting—though supremely strenuous—exercise in causal futility. *There may be "Absolute Truth" in the Essence of the Kabbalah. There is none in the psychological interpretation of Kabbalistic tenets, nor in the application of those interpretations to the practice of magic.* ***All*** *such interpretations and their application to magical practices are strictly* ***relative***. Yet it is also most certainly true that a ***general*** *understanding of the mind is absolutely necessary in order for the magician to avoid the traps of self-delusion and illusion, which the Magical Arts and Sciences produce in enormous abundance.*

To help the reader in this regard, I have provided a few of the better resources on the subject in the Recommended Reading List at the back of this book. The reader should find these recommended texts to be a great aid in acquiring that realistic, psychoanalytically-insightful and operational base necessary for one's understanding of themselves, their motivations in practicing magic, and in understanding the mind's effects on elementary to intermediate level magical practices.

As a consequence of point three above, the reader is cautioned to remember that the following Kabbalistic Analysis will be according to *my* state of subjective synthesis. I could write from no other point of view. Nevertheless, its content, process, and general overall procedure and structure will give the reader a fair idea of what Kabbalistic Analysis is all about, while providing the student of magic with a rigorous methodology needed to effectively do their own analyses.

Having provided the reader with some background on the salient issues underlying this work, we can now turn to the general process of Kabbalistic analysis, and the analysis of the Lesser Banishing Ritual of the Pentagram (LBRP) proper.

Kabbalistic Analysis of The Lesser Banishing Ritual of the Pentagram (LBRP)

The 'how' of the 'process' of Kabbalistic Analysis for Western Magic proceeds as follows:

The General Process of Kabbalistic Analysis

1. The magician identifies the particular branch or category of magic in which he or she will be working.

2. He or she determines the ritual act(s) or ceremonial performance(s) within that category or branch of magic that they will be performing.

3. The student studies the original Golden Dawn material as given in *The Complete Golden Dawn System of Magic* and compares it to *at least* one other published version of the work in order to understand the outline form behind the teachings and obtain a weighted average of the presentations, all the while making the appropriate notes thought relevant to the rite. He or she pays close attention to their inner promptings and the nagging questions that arise as they study.

The student is aware that these promptings are subconscious inducements needed by the deeper levels of the mind to bring about an ordered state of subjective synthesis regarding the particular ritual or ceremony being considered. The individual makes certain that any supporting material—such as that found in any of the appropriate Knowledge Lectures in the Golden Dawn book—is also understood to their conscious satisfaction. The magician works at this intellectual exercise until he or she feels right about it. This is an indication that the material has been accepted and properly fitted into their subconscious realm, and is site specific to the magic involved.

At this point, the individual rests assured, knowing they do not have to concern themselves with the material being properly fitted in with their overall state of subjective synthesis. They know that this latter process will follow of its own accord as they work diligently, consistently, and carefully in acquiring the knowledge that produces this right feeling within them.

4. Now the student thoroughly studies the corresponding material of the ritual act or ceremonial performance in *The Ritual Magic Manual,* since the actual performance will be according to those applied—yet rigorous—instructions given in this manual. Additional appropriate notes—especially those the magician feels prompted to make—are written out in full, as the details of the rite are studied from this book. All questions surfacing in the mind of the practitioner are noted, regardless of how absurd, foolish, or dumb they may seem. In so doing, the individual is once again reminded of the ancient maxim that the only foolish question is the one not asked.

5. The magician now reads corresponding sections of *The Three Books of Occult Philosophy.* Since this is thought to be the major source material from which most if not all of the Golden Dawn writings (albeit originally and partially pirated by Francis Barrett and placed into his 1801 edition of *The Magus,* which was later used by Mathers, Westcott, and Woods to produce the original Golden Dawn material) were obtained, it is essential that the reader understand the importance of the work as it appeared in the legitimate source material of the *Three Books* ascribed to Henry Cornelius Agrippa von Nettesheim. You will be surprised at the insights and understanding you will gain from a comparative study of corresponding ritual or ceremonial material from this book.

6. Refer to the appropriate chapter in this *Kabbalistic Handbook for the Practicing Magician* for the Kabbalistic information that pertains to that branch or category of magic in which you intend

to work. Look for those pieces of information that seem to answer the questions you gleaned from reading *The Complete Golden Dawn System of Magic,* at least one other published version of this material, *The Ritual Magic Manual,* and *The Three Books of Occult Philosophy.* Correlate those ideas and insights provided by the Kabbalah, and be certain that you write them out in full. That is, write them out as **tentative answers** to those questions you previously wrote down from your reading of the three books cited above.

Study these answers carefully. Ask yourself whether these Kabbalistic explanations or insights answer the questions to your satisfaction? Most importantly, ask yourself whether these answers feel right inside, or whether you are just going through the motions of this analysis so you can get on with the 'real' work? Make **certain** you are **honest** with yourself here, because if you do a slipshod job, looking only to get on with the 'real' work of magic, I *guarantee* you, your results will be in *direct proportion* to the effort you made in your analysis. Whether they like it or not, the practitioner will soon find out that this analysis is *the first real part* of that real magic the magician wants so desperately to perform.

After your Kabbalistic Analysis is complete—question by question, ritual or ceremonial component by component—sit back, review all of the material very carefully, and see how you feel about it. That is:

- What are your first intellectual reactions to your analysis?
- Is it complete?
- Does it answer each and every question to your conscious satisfaction?
- Are you absolutely certain you now have a handle on the ritual or ceremony, and what each and every part of it means in terms of your *relative* understanding? If so, good! You have traveled light years in developing or further strengthening your state of subjective synthesis on the particular magical ritual or ceremony that is the object of your analysis.

7. Now comes the hard part. Spend several days—a week or more if possible—feeling your way through your analysis. In other words, allow your forming subjective synthesis to effect the intellectual evaluation of your efforts by quietly contemplating the

material you have before you. Don't push your mind or force your conscious attention to detail. Let your intuition take over. You will find that some of the answers you thought were perfect no longer apply, and need further work. Others that continued to nag at you after your analysis was complete have suddenly been filled in for you, and this time, correctly. You can feel they are right now. Or, you may find that your original conscious, intellectual evaluation of the analysis stands as solid as a rock, only to have been shorn up by your contemplation, and made that much more clear by your intuitive gleanings. Regardless of the case, your time, attention to detail—at first—followed by your dismissal of detail—later—will weave a magical tapestry within you relative to the ritual or ceremonial practice you intend to perform. And you can rest assured it will work. And oh, how it will work!

8. Finally, you are now ready for what I call the Inner Perception and Magical Movement: The Dry Run Test. The reader might be amazed at how much magic goes bad or wrong because the magician is either unaware of, or simply and conveniently overlooks this simple sub-process of magical working. From my experience, it accounts for more disastrous ritual attempts, and the onset of the inevitable slingshot effect I discussed at length in my earlier book on Ceremonial Magic, than one cares to imagine.

Essentially, in this Dry Run Test, the student first performs the actions that the phrase implies. However, much, much more will eventually happen than would normally be expected from a normal practice run. Armed with the intellectual knowledge of the ritual or ceremony, and supported by knowing that a thorough Kabbalistic Analysis has been conducted, the practitioner enters the Temple, and *practices* performing the rite. Typically, the magical elemental weapons—if they have been made previously—are *not* used in the dry run, for obvious reasons. Practice the movements of the ritual with makeshift instruments, such as a wooden dowel or other representations of the elemental ritual weapon(s) to be used in the actual rite. Along with the practice of the physical movements, intonation (or vibration as Western Magic purists insist) of the divine names that will be employed in the actual ritual are also practiced. In addition, any mental imagery is also added. For example, visualization of any lineal figures that might be drawn in the air, the colors they are to be imaged in, the composition of circles, and whatever other images the actual rite calls for, are also thoroughly rehearsed.

Now, a curious set of events will be found to occur as more dry runs are continued over several days. Awkward movements and a self-conscious performance, normal in any new situation, will gradually fade. More specifically, the physical movements of the rite and the intonation of the appropriate divine names will begin to flow naturally, easily, and effectively. Any visualizations will seem to take on a reality of their own. This is as it should be. However, if there had been no Kabbalistic Analysis (coupled with building and strengthening one's state of subjective synthesis), this is about as far as the practitioner will progress in the rite performance.

The ritual effort will consequently be a hollow thing, lacking the energy, vitality, and vivifying power that can only be granted to the ritual or ceremony by the Kabbalistic forces flowing through the subconscious mind of the practitioner. That is, no matter how many times the ritual is performed, or how many divine names are vibrated from the Temple roof top, and despite the intended earnestness, the effort will be a feeble one at best. And as with an empty shell, so too will be the vacuous results of such performance(s).

However, since the practitioner has done a thorough Kabbalistic Analysis of the ritual or ceremony, and has worked diligently and consistently to build up and strengthen his or her subconscious state of subjective synthesis on the ritual, something else will begin to occur after the self-consciousness and awkwardness fade. The Inner Perception and Magical Movement part of this process will automatically take over.

As the practice continues—usually on the third day—the physical movements become surreal. In the case of the LBRP used in the example to follow, the magician begins to almost see the pentagrams in the air. They are not actually present, of course. Rather, it will feel as if they are almost there. It is as if a very thin, invisible shade is blocking their physical presence. As soon as the magician experiences this inner state, this perception will turn outward from the mind into the ritual chamber. He or she will suddenly understand in a nebulous yet intimately personal way, that the pentagrams are not simply some projected mental construct being forced from one's mind into the physical, lineal movements that trace the pentagram figures in the air.

What is happening? *The Astral World is merging with the physical world in which the practical performance is taking place, and genuine Astral Vision is being developed in the magician.* An overlap or tunnel between the two worlds is being established, and this is exactly what the magician wants. The psychic faculty of Clairvoyance has been stimulated, and one's Inner Perception is now at work. The vision of the pentagrams becomes so incredibly real that while the magician knows they are not physically present in the air in front of them, it will nevertheless seem as if the figures could be touched with the outstretched hand. And when the divine names are intonated—whether pronounced or vibrated aloud—the intonation will be spoken *automatically and naturally* with such power, that the practitioner will think something or someone else is behind or within them, issuing forth the holy names.

If an objective outside observer were in the Temple with the magician during this time, that observer would not find the vocalizations to be at all loud. Yet to the inner perceptions and [now] activated psychic faculty of Clairaudience, the magician will feel as if the Veils of Existence have been torn asunder. **THIS** is the power; the life; the vivifying force brought to the rite by the Kabbalah, and by the subconscious state of subjective synthesis of which I speak. Can the reader imagine what results such a simple ritual performance as that of the LBRP will now create, both within the psychic nature of the magician and in his or her external, worldly environment? If not—and if the practitioner follows the instructions in this Handbook—they soon will!

Even in the case of such a simple, preparatory ritual as the LBRP, after another day or two of dry run practice, certain other phenomena will commence. The magician will begin to experience sights and sounds in the Temple. In the beginning, faint whispers will arise that at first will startle. Flashes of light will follow next, seeming to emanate from empty space in the room. This will be followed by the appearance of small, angelic or humanoid figures cloaked in a gray or a diffused white garb, standing on the *inside* of the circle, with the entities becoming more and more real as the magician's Astral Vision continues to develop.

They will have no faces. But their presence will bring about a tremendous peace in the practitioner, and a joy that cannot be explained, but only experienced. And yet, there will be a sense of undulating power flowing from them; a power whose potential is beyond our normal understanding of the word frightening. Finally, light breezes or gusts of air will arise in the chamber, even though there may be no windows in the room. If windows are present and they have been tightly shut and sealed off, it will make no difference. The winds will still come.

Whether all or some of these phenomena are physically, empirically present, or are entering through the magician's astral senses, makes no difference. They are *real*. As real as are any of the other levels of existence that Quantum Physics has established as fact: matter and energy are indeed quite interchangeable.

Then it will happen. During one of the magician's dry runs, there will no longer be the ritualist, and the ritual movements. There will only be the ritual. There will be no difference between the practitioner and the practice. If the reader has ever experienced this Zen-like state, this is when it will occur. That which was two, has become one. And in that one, all power flows, and is directed by the consciousness and Will of the magician. *THIS* is *REAL Magic*! When you experience this, your subjective synthesis for this particular ritual—whether the LBRP to be examined here or another, more complex ritual or ceremony—has taken effect in the deepest levels of your mind. You are now ready for the actual ritual performance. And what a performance it will be!

In the particular example of the LBRP to follow next, the combination of astral expansion induced by the Qabalistic Cross; the tracing of the lineal figures in the air—without a magical weapon during the dry runs and with an elemental weapon during the actual performance(s); the mental imaging of the figures and intonation of the divine names; all will produce inner psychic states and real world results that will astound the practitioner at first. I dwell on this point to encourage the reader to take these instructions and admonitions on performing the Kabbalistic Analysis **seriously**. Imagine. If you follow my counsel, this will only be the beginning of your *real* magical work, and its attendant results.

Consider this also. *If* this very basic ritual of the LBRP produces such effects, what will other, more elaborate, complex rituals produce—*if* you follow through with your Kabbalistic training, analyses, and the development of your subconscious state of subjective synthesis? I think the reader now has a very clear idea as to what those results can and will be.

Thus, you will come to understand *from your own experience* that there is no need to psychologize by following the latest fad school of psychological thought, imported into the New Age by its subscribers, designed to soothe their fears of that which they cannot understand, nor hope to grasp. Neither will you need to provide a rigid psychological interpretation, or in other words, a rationalization, explanation, or worst of all, an acceptable reason for your magical failures, because these too have happened to you already—as you so very well know.

But most important of all, you will not have to resort to the insane spiritual pretenses of New Age dandies, who parade the need for initiation at the hands of other mortal men and women, while wearing the badges of their Grades high for all lower ranking Order members to see and pay homage to, before those same 'lower' members can experience 'genuine magical wonders.'

You will not need to pretend that your voice carried out to the furthest ends of Creation. You will not need to sully yourself with the self-lie that you really 'heard' the roar of God within your own voice. You will *know* it from your *experience* of it. Nor will you need to rationalize that you truly are as a gigantic being, whose physical eyes—now wide opened after the Qabalistic Cross component part of the LBRP—stare down at the floor of your Temple, perhaps only six feet away from your physical eyes as the yardstick measures, but which truly feel to be one with the position of your astral eyes, trillions of miles away, situated in your enormously expanded astral head that engulfs galaxies at the end of Creation.

You will not need the constructs, self-illusions and excuses of your New Age contemporaries who use such ploys to explain away their magical failures, because you will have experienced directly for yourself, that which they can only mouth. This is only the first Gift of *all* True Magic, regardless of its era—and this includes Western Magic—when **properly** performed.

Kabbalistic Analysis Proper of the LBRP
A Cautionary Note

As I mentioned in the Course Content section of this chapter, please be acutely aware that there are several different publishers of the Golden Dawn material that appeared in the original four volume set. Each republished version has been revised and enlarged to one extent or another, material rearranged, commentaries added, and some have even—yes, believe it or not—attempted to streamline the original information to fit the prevailing New Age view that magic 'evolves.'

As the reader will eventually discover, magic does *not* evolve. Human understanding of its tenets *change*, and owing to the general psychological makeup of human nature, that change usually heads into a deleterious, point-and-click mentality direction. In such change, knowledge is replaced by conjectures; hard work, by quick fixes; depth understanding, by brief explanations. In still other instances, 're-interpretations' of the original material have produced instructions that are almost unrecognizable when compared to the original source documents.

This being the case, *I once again strongly suggest that the reader acquaint him or herself with—at the very least—two or more of these different versions of Golden Dawn magical instructions in order to obtain as comprehensive a view of the material as is possible. That is, a weighted average, as I previously mentioned.* Even though the original Golden Dawn material, as presented in the original 1937–1940 publication, still constitutes a patched together, inharmonious eclectic effort as I contend, the system presented in the different versions available today makes this attempt at eclecticism even more difficult. Thus, it is best the reader be aware of the variations that have been written into the original writings, by making the comparisons suggested.

Also, please be aware that owing to these numerous variations, the Kabbalistic Analysis of the Lesser Banishing Ritual of the Pentagram to be given in this section, will be a *proximal version* to the mean, thus mirroring many of the variations the reader will find in that ritual, depending upon the actual version of the Golden Dawn book or Golden Dawn ritual instructions used. In so doing, I trust the reader will also be able to obtain a grounding in just how to obtain this weighted average of these variations, regardless of the Golden Dawn type, or other Western magical ritual or ceremonial work for that matter, they intend to undertake in their private practice.

Kabbalistic Analysis Applied to
The Lesser Banishing Ritual of the Pentagram (LBRP)

1. The practitioner has determined that the category of magic he or she will be working in is that of the Preparatory Magical Practices.

2. He or she has determined that the ritual to be mastered is that of the LBRP.

3. The practitioner has carefully studied the corresponding background information on the ritual—for instance, the applicable Knowledge Lecture material—as well as the ritual directions from at least two different versions of available Golden Dawn texts. He or she has paid close attention to the internal promptings that have arisen within them as they studied the material, and made copious notes regarding those questions and concerns that arose during the study. The practitioner has also taken pains to make certain they understand the material to their complete satisfaction.

4. After studying the corresponding ritual material from *The Ritual Magic Manual,* the student may have uncovered further questions and—as in the case of their Golden Dawn review—has written out these questions in full. Some tentative answers to the Golden Dawn questions in step 3. may even have surfaced by this time, and have been written down. Perhaps some insight as to the application of Kabbalah in answering a number of these or other queries, has also occurred by now. If so, fine. If not, they will come as the individual continues the Kabbalistic Analysis.

5. The magician now researches those corresponding sections of *The Three Books of Occult Philosophy* in order to achieve some understanding of the source material from which the ritual components were derived. At this point the practitioner should not be surprised to find a wealth of answers to their original questions produced by steps 3. and 4., finding their way up to consciousness. This is the function of the *Three Books*: to deepen one's understanding, and to clarify issues. ***Pay close attention to the original material set down (supposedly) by Agrippa, and carefully distinguish it from the commentaries and annotations of its***

Editor. Not that the Editor's comments are in error or inconsequential in any way. Far from it! Rather, it is always more helpful to learn and understand the thoughts, instructions, and interpretations of the author (in this case, the text purportedly written by Agrippa), before expanding that understanding through a study of the interpretations and opinions of another, no matter how insightful and correct they may be (here, the Editor of the *Three Books*).

6. At this juncture, the practitioner may have organized the process of the LBRP into something like that given below. He or she now begins to study the Kabbalistic section of this Handbook, looking for answers, while correlating such information with his or her own ideas, insights, and tentative conclusions, all of which have arisen due to their growing understanding of the theology of the Kabbalah. Some answers will fall in place. Yet other questions will arise, and additional tentative conclusions surface. Still others will require backtracking and restudying the Golden Dawn and other related material. Remember. Kabbalistic Analysis is a process, and as such, moves back and forth between a question/answer/insight and further question/further insight procedure, until a 'final answer' is achieved, and a feeling of 'rightness' is attained. It takes time. But as the reader will find, that time will be well spent.

(Once again, please remember: The pattern of the ritual's organization and the brief example questions that follow—and they are by no means complete!—are according to my subconscious state of subjective synthesis. The reader's organizational pattern and question-type will no doubt be quite different. Also be aware that I am painfully conscious the analysis given below may be considered by some—or even, by many—to be unnecessarily rigorous, while no doubt, complaints of my being pedantic are sure to arise from others.

Be that as it may, this process *works*, and works profoundly each time it is used, in terms of the ritual or ceremonial *results achieved.* As always, it is up to the reader to determine just how far he or she will go in these things and therefore just how complete their ritual and ceremonial results will be! The choice is *yours*!)

The practitioner now continues his or her depth analysis proper:

Ok. I have determined that the LBRP can be essentially broken down into three separate and distinct phases, each of which has additional aspects to it. So to make this as easy on myself as possible, I'm going to list those three phases and the various aspects of each, and pose my questions for each phase and its aspects as I go along. Then I'm going to see if I can derive some answers to those questions by applying the Kabbalah. In so doing, I intend to achieve a better understanding of the entire process of the LBRP than I now possess, while furthering my grasp of the Kabbalah, not to mention building up and strengthening my subconscious state of subjective synthesis. I know it's going to be quite a job, applying the hard data of the Kabbalah to all of this, but if that's what it takes to get the results that I want from my ritual and ceremonial work, then so be it.

A. **Phase One**—The Kabbalistic Cross used to 'Open the Temple Proper'

1) Astral expansion of my astral form until I encompass the universe, and Kether is directly above my enormously expanded, astral head.

2) I draw down the Light of Kether through my enormous astral head with a hand gesture, in order to bring this Light down through my astral body—as well as through my physical form—until it reaches my feet. I accomplish this by touching my forehead, breast, and groin as I direct this shaft of White Light down to an infinitesimally small earth and beyond.

a) I intone the word, "ATH" or "ATAH" (Hebrew, meaning "Thou" and pronounced "Thou art"). "A (ah)" is pronounced upon touching my forehead, "T (tā)" upon touching my breast, and "H(ah)" upon touching my groin. "Malkuth" (meaning, "Kingdom" pronounced "the Kingdom") is intoned after touching the groin, and as I image the shaft of Light descending into Malkuth and beyond.

b) Now I image the completely descended vertical shaft of the pure, brilliant, Divine White Light of Spirit as being suffused throughout my expanded astral body and corresponding—by contrast— miniature physical body.

3) Now it is time to formulate the horizontal arm of the Cross. I begin by touching my right shoulder, and imaging a brilliant sphere of White Light forming just off of it. A shaft of White Light jets out from this sphere, penetrates through my right shoulder, and joins the vertical shaft of Light at a point within my chest, while another shaft of this Light from this sphere extends outward, to my right, to the furthermost reaches of the universe: out to infinity itself. As I perform this movement and image the shafts of Light, I intone, "Ve Geburah" (meaning "The Power," and pronounced "and the Power").

4) The formulation of the left horizontal arm of the Cross is now carried out by touching my left shoulder, and imaging another brilliant sphere of White Light forming just off of it. A shaft of this Light is then projected from this sphere—as in the case of the sphere formed off of my right shoulder—which penetrates through my left shoulder, and joins with the shaft of vertical White Light at a point within my chest. At the same time, another shaft of White Light extends outward from this new sphere of White Light, to my left, and travels out to the furthermost reaches of infinity. As I carry out this movement, I intone, "Ve Gedulah" (meaning "The Glory" and pronounced, "and the Glory").

5) I now complete the process of the Kabbalistic Cross by clasping both hands on my chest as I intone, "Le Olam" (meaning, "Forever"), Amen (meaning, "So Be It").

Possible Kabbalistic Considerations and Questions for **Phase One** *and its various aspects:* I am obviously expanding my astral form through the Middle Pillar of the Tree of Life until I reach a point just below Kether. Is this act symbolic of the ascent spoken of in the Golden Dawn and other magical sources, by which 'Manhood ascends to God Head, and God Head descends into Manhood'? What exactly are the correspondences of Malkuth, the Sephirah in which I live daily, and which I think I am attempting to elevate through this magical effort? I know them *generally*. But I mean, what are they precisely? What are they, *Really*?

I never dwelt upon them before to any extent. Are these correspondences of Malkuth strictly physical? Or, since Malkuth is directly connected to Hod, Yesod, and Netzach by the 31st, 32nd, and 29th Paths respectively, are the mental, psychic, and material correspondences of these three Sephiroth also being elevated as well, *through* their active role in Malkuth? What are the forces operating behind these Paths, anyway? And if they are being elevated toward Divinity, am I attempting something more through this simple 'Opening of the Temple Proper' than at first appears? Am I also attempting to elevate my overall humanness toward that One Divine Essence—the Yechidah—the highest aspect of my own soul, which is a component of my Neshamah? And if I am, and since the Neshamah is one of the higher aspects of my own soul as well, and corresponds to the third Sephirah, Binah, what relation does this part of my nature have to the overall process of astral expansion and the Kabbalistic Cross?

Could it be that since the Neshamah—this supernal understanding—is one of the three components of my soul, the other two being the Chiah and the Yechidah itself, that I am attempting to elevate my human nature to unite with all three? Am I building another 'Cross of Light' then, between the correspondences of the Yechidah, the Chiah, and the Neshamah? In other words, between Kether, Chokmah, and Binah, respectively, as well? Since these three parts of my soul—the Yechidah, the Chiah and the Neshamah—are above the Abyss and constitute my own Higher and Divine Genius, am I preparing myself to eventually unite with that Higher and Divine Genius by this act? And if so, where? Above the Abyss, or at some point below the Abyss, seeing that the 'Crossing of the Abyss' involves the annihilation of my own ego, and yet is the 'Summit Achievement' in any spiritual discipline, including that of magic?

Or could it be that *a* uniting—a sort of 'preamble' to this Crossing—will occur below the Abyss, by my Attaining to the K&C of my HGA in Tiphareth? And am I symbolically building this latter 'Lesser Attainment' into my practice of the Kabbalistic Cross, while at the same time seeding my highest aspiration for the Crossing itself? After all, by touching my breast and intoning the "T (tā)" in ATH (ATAH) as I draw down the White Light of Kether, I am certainly acknowledging Tiphareth—the realm of the HGA.

What are the essential correspondences and connecting implications then, of Kether, Binah, and Tiphareth, in this act of performing the Kabbalistic Cross? In fact, what are the esoteric implications here of Chokmah also, since it corresponds to the Chiah? Do I dare consider questions of the Paths and their meanings between these four Sephiroth? That is, the Paths between Kether, Chokmah, Binah, and Tiphareth, as well? And what of the Path between Tiphareth and Yesod? Since I touch the genitals while intoning "H (ah)," I am obviously bringing Yesod, the Moon, and the subconscious into the overall performance as well? Come to think of it, what are the correspondences—mundane, esoteric, and magical—of Yesod?

And something else. I am only openly acknowledging Geburah and Chesed by touching my right and left shoulders respectively, as I trace out the Cross upon my astral form and physical body. Why? To be sure, Geburah and Chesed are below the Abyss. Am I then *also* creating a 'Cross of Light' within the material *and* astral worlds, thereby establishing a portal through which the Kabbalistic power and magical force of these two Sephiroth and their planetary correspondences can flow? Power and force that will enable me to effect the gross matter in Malkuth—that is, to attain my material desires through magical ends—while yet aspiring to the Attainment of the K&C of the HGA, and still expressing a spiritual impulse for the eventual Summit Attainment?

Am I therefore seeking to establish a balance of purpose and intent between the material and spiritual (or psychic) realms, as well? What then, are the correspondences of Geburah and Chesed that might support or deny these assumptions of mine? Will I find them explicitly stated in the Kabbalistic chapter of this book, or in the further study of the Kabbalah? Or will I have to intuit the answers to these insights after I have sufficiently built up my state of subconscious synthesis?

After all, as this author stated, when it comes to Kabbalistic knowledge and building up one's own subconscious state of subjective synthesis in magical matters, not only does one size fits all not apply, but he also reminds us that while there may be Absolute Truth in the Essence of Kabbalah, there is none in the psychological interpretation of Kabbalistic tenets, nor in the application of those interpretations to the practice of magic. As he stated, all is relative.

Another thing. As I go through the Kabbalistic material, searching out some answers and intuiting others, I am going to force myself—if necessary—to keep the following questions always in the forefront of my mind. Do the Kabbalistic explanations, conclusions, and insights I have derived from my study, truly answer my questions to my satisfaction? That is, do these answers 'feel right inside' where it counts? Or am I just going through the motions of this analysis, so I can get on with the 'real' work? I have to be completely honest with myself here, *if* my magic is to work the way I want it to!

(These are only a few of the possible questions that might arise in the magician's mind during the analysis. Nevertheless, they show the complexity that can easily enter into this process. Additionally, they should serve to give the reader a clearer understanding of the importance in building up, strengthening, and ordering his or her subconscious state of subjective synthesis through such analysis.)

B. **Phase Two**—The Tracing of the Pentagram Lineal Figures in the Air, and the Summoning of the Archangels.

Hmmm. This phase of the LBRP seems quite complex. Much more so than the Kabbalistic Cross. I think it would be better if I break this phase up into a few different parts, list the aspects for each part, and then pose my Kabbalistic considerations and questions.

B. **Phase Two: Part I**

1) I move to the east and trace the lineal figure of a Banishing Pentagram in the air with my finger or makeshift 'weapon' (at first). Later, after the Inner Perception and Magical Movement: The Dry Run Test, I'll use the actual ritual weapon, of course. I image the Pentagram to be hovering in the air, an arm's length away from me, in a brilliant, flaming blue light. The Pentagram doesn't 'become' blue. Rather, from its Earth-point of origin back to its Earth-point of comple-

tion, I image it in this flaming blue light as I trace it in the air. In other words, at first, I'll simply be 'projecting' it from my finger or makeshift weapon as I sweep out its lines and vertices.

Further, after studying the complete ritual, I notice the same procedures are used in each quarter. That is, a similar Pentagram is traced in the air in the south, west, and north quadrants respectively, and in order to do this, I am to rotate about my own axis clockwise—or 'deosil'—in order to trace each one.

Possible Kabbalistic Considerations and Questions for **Phase Two, B, Part I.** Ok. I recognize that the five angles of each Pentagram corresponds to the Five Elements, Fire, Earth, Air, and Water, the top point being assigned to Spirit. I also know that color schemes are part of the Elemental attributions. That is, red is assigned to Fire; russet or olive, citrine, or black depending upon what I'm doing—to Earth; yellow or violet, to Air; and blue to Water. Spirit takes the presence of all colors, harmoniously united into what we call the color white.

So why are the Pentagrams of the Lesser Banishing Ritual of the Pentagram to be imaged in a blue light? Am I invoking the Water Element here? How can this be, since I am banishing from the Earth point of the Pentagram to the angle of Spirit, and finishing back at the angle of the Earth Element? This doesn't make any sense. If I am banishing from the starting point of Earth and thereby banishing by Earth, shouldn't the Pentagrams be black? Or even, olive, or russet, or maybe even citrine? Boy, I don't know what to think here! None of the books on the Golden Dawn or any other magical material I've seen address this or other such Kabbalistic issues! Guess I'll have to figure it out for myself, Kabbalistically. Intuit it, like this author said. Ok, so for the time being then, I'll leave this question alone and go on. Maybe some insight will pop up later.

B. Phase Two: Part II

1) Now, after I trace out the first Pentagram in the east, I am to stab the center of it with my finger or weapon, and keep my arm outstretched as I rotate to the south, deosil. Fair enough. However, one Golden Dawn book states that I am to image a line of *white light* connecting the center of the Pentagram in the east with the center

of the Pentagram about to be drawn in the south. The same procedure is to be used in connecting the final two Pentagrams after I trace them out. That is, the third one, traced in the west, is to be connected by this white line, as will be the fourth one in the north. Finally, I'm to complete the circle by connecting the Pentagram in the north with the original one in the east, by sweeping an arc from the center of the north Pentagram back to the one in the east, always moving deosil.

Possible Kabbalistic Considerations and Questions for **Phase Two, B, Part II.** All well and good. But what is this white light business? I noticed that in the 1969 second edition of the Golden Dawn, it states, "When tracing the Pentagrams, the imagination should be exerted to visualize them as flaming stars all about one. The impression should be of a *fire ring* studded in four places with stars of flame."[8] Unless I'm really off base here, a 'ring of fire' would be red in color, not white! Still yet another source states that the circle connecting the Pentagrams is to be a blue color! Why the variations? Am I being too picky? Am I reading things into this that are not here?

(Later) No, I'm not being too picky. Not by a long shot. These questions arose in my mind, and by doing so, they demand an answer. One that will feel right when I get it. So in keeping with this author's counsel, I've mulled this over, and looked deep within myself. I've felt my way through this matter, and am absolutely certain. They must be answered, and to my satisfaction! Nor am I reading anything into this concern that isn't really there. How do I know? *Because color has Kabbalistic significance.* And since it does, it must invoke different Sephiroth and their correspondences. So how do I analyze this?

Wait! It just occurred to me. Blue Pentagrams and a ring of fire. Blue is obviously invoking the attributes of Chesed, while red—the color of an intense fire—takes correspondences of Geburah! And come to think of it, those are the two Sephiroth I am formulating off of my shoulders to form the horizontal arm of the Kabbalistic Cross! So the starting angle from the Earth point is just that: a beginning point by which I am declaring my purpose, which is to banish by Earth, since that point is assigned to the Element, Earth!

Tracing out the Pentagrams has nothing to do with the color attributions of the Elements! That is, the starting point for tracing out a Pentagram simply invokes the power of that Element! So, the color correspondences here must be symbolic representations of Geburah and Chesed—at least in this ritual—and therefore of Mars and Jupiter, which I am thus 'declaring' or invoking in the ritual! So I am not simply 'formulating' them in the horizontal arm of the Cross of Light by imaging them across my body. *I am actually invoking their force by bringing them down into the ritual, and 'balancing' them by using their color schemes in both the color of the Pentagrams, and in the 'ring of fire' connecting them!* What a powerful magical statement!

That's it! Now I've got it! This business of connecting the Pentagrams by a ring of white light makes no sense at all—to *me*! If I did use white light for the ring here, I'd be invoking the power of Spirit, which is just plain weird in this instance! Uh uh. No way. It just doesn't feel right, and there is no Golden Dawn text that I can find to explain or support it being done in the color white. Maybe one of those New Age ideas this author is so dead set against? That does it.

For *me*, the Pentagrams of the LBRP will be traced out and imaged in the blue light of Chesed and Jupiter, and the circle connecting all four will be imaged in red—as is the color correspondence of Geburah and Mars. Balance all around. Now I **understand**! Could this be the beginning of building *my* personal state of subjective synthesis? That subconscious condition this guy has been talking about here? I darn well bet it is!

And maybe I'd better investigate the meanings of the 19th Path between Geburah and Chesed also, because this feels so right to me, I can't escape it! And oh, how appropriate too, the 19th Path—The Path of Strength! It's all beginning to make sense now! Especially since that white light business for the circle doesn't have any direct Path connection between Kether, Geburah and Chesed. Hence there is no Kabbalistic reason whatsoever in using the white light color for this crucial ritual component—the connecting ring—at least, none that I can find. And intuiting it tells me it's wrong, to boot. And certainly, that's what the implication of the white light is in this instance, as I thought: bringing Spirit into the ritual. It may sound good at first, but as I see it, it's just not Kabbalistically correct. And after all, that's what Western

Magic is all about—the Kabbalah and its *knowledgeable application* to ritual and ceremonial performances—or, that's what it should be all about!

Since I have made this Path-implication discovery, I'd better bone up on the meanings of the 13th, 25th, and 32nd Paths as well, since they too are obviously being declared, and thus their force being invoked in this composite ritual. And what about Paths 20 and 22? What possible implication can they have in this ritual, since they are inferred by their direct connection to Tiphareth?

B. Phase Two: Part III
1) The other aspect of this ritual that has to be addressed Kabbalistically, is that of the Divine Names that are to be projected through each of the Pentagrams. In the east, the Name is YHVH, pronounced Yod-heh-vav-heh. In the south, ADNI, intonated as, Ah–doh–nai. In the west, AHIA, or, Eh–he–yeh, and in the north, AGLA, intoned as, Ah–ge–lah.

Possible Kabbalistic Considerations and Questions for **Phase Two, B, Part III:** Why? What is the significance of these Names in these quarters, for this particular ritual? I ask this, because I know there are many possible attributions assigned to them and to their component parts, depending upon the ritual or ceremony in which they are used, and in the specific part of a given rite in which they are employed, for that matter. So what do I have here?

Well, first of all, I notice that each Name consists of four letters in the original Hebrew. There are four Elements as well, since in mystical traditions, Spirit is sometimes considered an Element, and other times, it is not. Once again, it depends on what you're doing, magically. I remember from reading the Knowledge Lectures that each of these Names were assigned to a specific quarter for a specific reason, but the reasons weren't stated. At least, not explicitly that I could find. So I'd better do more digging, because this is certainly a very important point—to me.

I do know however, that in the case of the Pentagram in the east, the Divine Name, YHVH, represents the Four Elements which—under the symbol of the Cross—are ruled by the YHVH. I also know that the Pentagram is a powerful symbolic representation of the Four Elements and Spirit operating under the divine aegis of the letters of the Holy Name, Yeheshuah. What could this mean? Could this be a ritual declaration that all four Pentagrams are being placed under this presidency, while the other three are invoking yet other aspects of God's Nature? And what of these other three names? Why are they specific to each quarter? I'd better go more deeply into the Kabbalah chapters of this Handbook and into the Golden Dawn text. And it certainly wouldn't hurt to look into the Recommended Reading List at the back of this book. The answers have *got* to be in at least one of these resources!

B. **Phase Two: Part IV**

   1) And finally, do my deosil movements symbolically follow the movement of the sun, proclaim the cycle of Creation as given by the ancient maxim '...for he (the Sun) is true in his course from east to west, thereby showing the beginning, the proceedings, and ending of all things, as he crosseth the sphere of heaven in his daily labors...'? Some more work to do! As I said before, I'd better restudy the Kabbalah in this handbook more carefully this time, and see what I can find—explicitly stated. Or, maybe something that will allow me to feel my way; intuit the answer, as I've done before.

Possible Kabbalistic Considerations and Questions for **Phase Two, B, Part IV**: Really, I don't have any particular questions on this part of the rite—at least not yet. I think the supplementary reading will flesh out my understanding of this issue.

B. **Phase Two: Part V**

   1) This part of the ritual is clear to me: the imaging and calling upon the four mighty Archangels, Raphael, Michael, Gabriel, and Auriel, that are Kabbalistically assigned to the four quarters of the universe, according to the ancient maxim, '...as the winds blow.' I have researched their natures, am very well familiar with their characteristics and 'personalities,' know why I am calling upon them, and feel right internally, with this part of the ritual. So no problem here.

Possible Kabbalistic Considerations and Questions for **Phase Two, B, Part V**: None, really. I quite clear on everything here, feel right about it, and am quite confident I understand these matters perfectly.

C. **Phase Three—Kabbalistic Cross Used to 'Close the Temple Proper.'**
   1) The procedure of the Kabbalistic Cross is repeated as in A. Phase One. I understand this quite well now, and know that it's supposed to be used at this point in the LBRP to 'Close the Temple Proper.' BUT...!

*Possible Kabbalistic Considerations and Questions for **Phase Three**:* What is meant by 'Closing the Temple Proper'? For that matter, what is meant by 'Opening the Temple Proper'? This seemingly simple physical and imaging gesture is not as 'simple' as I found out from doing this analysis. Its hidden meanings are as astounding as are the Kabbalistic forces I am calling down by performing it! But why 'Opening' and 'Closing'? What could these mean? I have a feeling this part of the LBRP has a psychological component to it as well.

I recall reading something, somewhere, which dealt with using symbolic gestures as a means of gaining entrance into the subconscious realm, and then using similar or other gestures to extricate oneself from it. It was something about making certain the portal to the unconscious is under one's conscious control, so the unconscious content and forces don't break in upon one's everyday waking consciousness. Hmmm. Sounds like something Israel Regardie wrote in one of his books, so I'd better refresh myself with the ones on the Recommended Reading List here. It's sure to have it. In fact, come to think of it, I seem to recall that it's in that old copy of *The Twelve Steps to Spiritual Enlightment*[9] that Regardie wrote years ago! So I'd better check into it.

Then, too, I recall that excellent Introduction to the Llewellyn fifth and sixth editions of *The Golden Dawn*, written by Cris Monnastre.[10] Her insightful commentaries gave me much insight into the psychological basis of magic in general. I was very shaky on this part of things until I read her work. I think I'll reread those papers, and see where they take me. For now however, I'll accept the position that the Kabbalistic Cross not only has a powerful magical function in calling down the forces of the various Sephiroth, but has an important psychological importance as well, in that it bars me from unknowingly gate crashing into my subconscious mind. I'll flesh out these ideas as I continue this analysis.

And finally, I won't forget that the performance of this ritual gesture is to place myself under the aegis of my Higher and Divine Genius—or the Yechidah in me, as far as that confused term is used in the literature. Come to think of it, if I place myself under the shield and protection of my Yechidah at the beginning of the rite by performing the Kabbalistic Cross, and then perform this Kabbalistic Cross again at the Closing, I must actually be asking for the continuance of that protection and guidance after I return to my normal state of consciousness and go about my daily business. That's it! The Kabbalistic Cross then, also acts as a 'prayer,' by which I'm shielding and protecting myself: both during the ritual and in the altered states of consciousness the rite brings about, as well as afterward, when I go about my worldly business and am in my 'normal' state of consciousness! Wow! I never thought of this before! My understanding of the Kabbalistic Cross and its importance has just escalated a thousand percent!

Further Possible Kabbalistic Considerations and Questions for Phase Three: After just having this insight on a possible occult meaning of the Kabbalistic Cross to Open and Close the Temple Proper, I feel I'm alright with this part of the ritual. Nevertheless, I'm going to do that review I noted, and make certain the psychological aspects of this repeated component of the ritual are *thoroughly* understood by me!

(At this point of the Kabbalistic Analysis, the practitioner simply continues with the back-and-forth question and answer procedure until all questions are answered to his or her satisfaction, and—most importantly—that they feel right within them. After reaching this stage, he or she proceeds to step 7 in the process of analysis.)

7. After completing the analysis, the reader carries out two very necessary exercises. First, the intellectual approach is taken. He or she spends a few days restudying their completed analysis, and once more poses the questions: Is the analysis complete? I mean, am I certain I have addressed every question I had, or have I taken expedient short cuts and just 'played pretend' that I did the job to my own satisfaction? Do the Kabbalistic and intuited answers to my self-generated questions satisfy me? Do I truly

think I now have a handle on this particular ritual? Do I understand what each of its component parts mean? This is most important. Do not rush. Do not hurry.

Remember. You are building a personal and Kabbalistic edifice of resplendent beauty and enormous power within your own nature by taking these measures. Ask yourself, if I had the wherewithal to build the house of my dreams, would I short change myself by cutting corners here and there? Would I use plastic instead of steel? Fiberboard instead of oak? Outdoor carpeting instead of plush, comfortable pile? Cheaper wiring that could break down, catch fire, and destroy my dream house, or would I make certain I used the finest heavy duty electrical cable made? After all, I intend to spend the rest of my life in this magnificent structure! It will not only be my fortress from the daily insanities of the world, but a sanctuary in which I will be able to grow and develop, enjoy myself, and do what I will to do. It will be the most important (physical) part of my own personal universe! So I'd better do it right the first time—because in fact—I may not have a second chance!

And now the hard part comes. For secondly, the reader must now engage his or her intuitional faculties by spending at least several days—a week or more if at all possible—feeling their way through the analysis. By doing so, the magician will allow his or her forming subjective synthesis to effect the intellectual evaluation of their efforts by contemplating, quietly, the material in front of them. Don't force conscious attention to detail. Let the intuition take over.

By doing so, the practitioner will find that some of the answers they thought were perfect suddenly no longer apply, and need further work. Others that hounded the individual from the outset of the analysis will have been answered unexpectedly—and this time, correctly. The reader will just feel in his or her bones that now they are right. Or, it may be the magician will find that his or her original conscious, intellectual evaluation of the analysis stands as solid as a rock, and has now been strengthened and stabilized by their contemplation, having been made that much more clear by their intuitive gleanings.

Regardless of the case, your time, conscious attention to detail—at first—followed by your dismissal of detail—later—will combine to create a beautiful, artistically balanced and scientifically sound magical condition within you, relative to the ritual or ceremonial practice you intend to perform. And you can be certain the particular ritual that underwent the analysis will now work for you, and work for you beyond your greatest expectations!

8. Finally, you are now ready for the Inner Perception and Magical Movement: The Dry Run Test, spoken of earlier. Please, please remember, that so very much of magic goes bad or wrong because the magician is either unaware of, or simply and conveniently overlooks this simple sub-process of magical working. As I have noted, my own experience has shown me that failure to carry out this process accounts for more disastrous ritual attempts—as well as the onset of the inevitable and terrifying Slingshot Effect I discussed at length in *Ceremonial Magic and the Power of Evocation*—than the reader might care to imagine. At this point then, the practitioner should return to the earlier discussion of this all important step, read it carefully, and execute it to the best of his or her ability. The phenomena that will be produced from it alone will be more than that needed to convince the magician of what *real* magic can do!

Chapter Three

The Agrippa System of Planetary Hours of the Day and Night

The reader being familiar with the Occult, he or she is no doubt aware of some system of plotting the hours of the day and night. To be sure, there are many such systems in the literature of the field, the most commonly known and used today being the Rosicrucian Order (AMORC) system presented by H. Spencer Lewis in his book, *Self Mastery and Fate with the Cycles of Life*[11].

While this and other similar, popular systems are used by some members of the mystical community, they are hardly applicable to the practicing magician, either as a tool for daily life affairs, or in magical work. Why is this so? Because in both cases, the magical forces—and this obviously refers to the Kabbalistic forces that are the generators of such force—with which the practitioner comes into daily contact through their work produces a life stream of experience and perception unlike any other. 'Each unto his own' is appropriate here.

But in magical literature, there are even more such astrologically based systems as, for example, in the case of different Grimoires or Grammars of Magic. In this instance, different grimoires can require their own particular method of hourly calculation in order to successfully work from a particular text. Then too, there are considerations for the calculations of propitious times under which astrological, zodiacal, and planetary magical operations should be carried out. These times are determined according to either the Sidereal or Tropical Zodiac, the Sidereal being the most favored. In the Sidereal realm, the Rosicrucian Sidereal Zodiacal system is probably the best known.

In the long run, because the magician is deluged with such a plethora of possibilities, and in some cases requirements, he or she usually defers to not using any system whatsoever. At best, the practitioner usually ascribes to the principle they were taught in school: study (perform your daily rituals) at the same time each day. While the latter instance has favorable psychological advantages, it does not take advantage of the very planetary, astrological, or zodiacal forces that will empower one's ritual performances. In effect, the practitioner may feel good after the ritual work, but little or no results are produced when it comes to the bottom line. So what astrological system, if any, do we use in order to work this system? Fortunately, there is a remarkably easy solution to this problem.

In 1533, the *Three Books of Occult Philosophy*[3], attributed to the scholar and magician, Henry Cornelius Agrippa von Nettesheim, first appeared in print as a complete set in Cologne, Germany. In this massive, all important sourcebook of Magic and Occultism, the author discusses a system of hours of the day and night—along with their planetary rulers—that serves as the basis of today's so called Western Magic. Although it is accurate to call it Western Magic, I feel it has become too strongly wedded to New Age fad magic, which has greatly detracted from its universal usefulness.

Nevertheless, the system itself, as a system of calculations of the hours of the day and night, and the planetary designations assigned to those hours, are the most useful in performing one's daily magical regimen. Of course, this system can also be perfectly applied to the performance of Preparatory, Planetary, Invocational, Talismanic, Divinatory, Zodiacal, and Sephirotic Magic, and in all those cases where stringent time constraints for a particular ritual are not laid down by text. (In the case of Elemental, Enochian, and Path Working Magic, other time systems may well apply, and should be used as called for.) Thus, it is this system—*the Agrippa System of Hours of the Day and Night*—that I *strongly* recommend for the practitioner, as delineated above. Now, as to the system itself.

In Chapter XXXIV, Book II, **Of the True Motion of the Heavenly Bodies to be Observed in the Eighth Sphere, and of the Ground of Planetary Hours** of *The Three Books of Occult Philosophy*, an accurate and precise exposition of the astrological principles of magic in both theory and application is laid down. This two-page chapter *effectively* explains that the astrologers of the time were committing a fundamental error by dividing the day (sunrise to sunset) into twelve equal periods.

Agrippa (if he was indeed the author of this splendid, complex source book of Western Magic) refers to such an invention as an "artificial hour." Additionally, the hours of the night (sunset to sunrise) were obtained with the same method. (Note also, how a much more grievous, inaccurate variation of this erroneous system is in use throughout the world today in determining what time it is.)

In a difficult fashion, his text argues that these twelve equal segments of day and night hours are not to be divided into twelve equal parts, but rather, "...so also in planetary hours the ascensions of fifteen degrees in the ecliptic constituteth an unequal or planetary hour, whose measure we ought to inquire and find out by the tables of oblique ascensions of every region."[12]

This is suggested as a more favorable division of the hours of the day and night into sections of unequal lengths, depending on the astronomical requirement stated in the quotation and is in answer to the equal hour division which the author acknowledges but does not favor as he states, "...for as in artificial hours, which are always equal to themselves, the ascensions of fifteen degrees in the equinoctial constituteth an artificial hour;..."[13] You can see the problem. If we use the more favorable division we would have to be profound astrologers to the nth degree, continuously calculating and recalculating for each daily ritual!

In effect, adopting *any* coherent, readily usable hourly system for magical working would be utterly impossible. In such a case the practitioner would literally have to resort to either using no system at all, or else would have to defer to the school study concept of the same time each day. The result in either case? The individual would have to muddle through ritual work and the paltry or negative results that would attend those ritual performances as best as they could. This is unfortunately what most people involved in Western Magic do. No. This is not the way to proceed with the Holy Work.

In my opinion, the author of the *Three Books* was actually suggesting that such *rigorous* astronomical observances are to be confined to major ritual and ceremonial magical practices, not to the daily magical work regimen, or to more common magical acts of an Invocational, Planetary, Talismanic, Divinatory, Zodiacal, or even Sephirothal nature.

Once again—and it is only my opinion—it was Agrippa's understanding of both sides of the coin that eventually gave rise to the system of artificial hours as they are applied in Occult and Magical work today, and which are indeed used to invoke the Kabbalistic forces that vitalize and vivify our magical practices. If the reader carefully studies the *Three Books*, making notes and comparing Agrippa's further explanations and doctrine, it is my feeling he or she will arrive at the same conclusion I have that these 'artificial hours' are truly magical hours and are astronomical in nature, as is indirectly argued for and defended in the *Three Books*.

Indeed, these hours are not based on the progressive movements of the hands on any watch or clock, whose accepted convention of marking time is a complete fabrication of social expediency. Instead, these magical hours are not sixty-minutes in length. Rather, they are based upon the time between sunrise and sunset, and sunset and sunrise, which of course changes on a daily basis.

I can hear the reader asking just how these hourly periods are calculated and whether all this is even necessary? You may accept the fact that Kabbalistic forces can vitalize the rituals, but doubt whether all of these ideas and instructions are absolutely essential and imperative.

My answer, of course, is that yes, all of these ideas and instructions are absolutely essential and imperative, *for reasons you will come to understand as you work with them, and apply them to your magical work.* In answer to the first question, the calculations are extremely simple, and require no more mathematics than addition, subtraction, multiplication, and division. A simple handheld calculator will suffice, as long as it has at least a single memory cell to store one piece of data, and no more. Now, onto answering some of your other silent, secret concerns.

The Reason for Calculating the Hours of the Day and Night

Cycles appear as frequencies or patterns of repetition everywhere in Nature. From the change of seasons, to a change in your sleep pattern; from the frequency of the electricity coming through your electrical wall outlet, to the beat of your heart. Cycles—and an innumerable number of other rhythms—are *the* fundamental *basis* of Nature, not simply just some part of it. From Babylon to Egypt to Greece, the early astrologers hammered out and synthesized a *practical*, useful eclectic system, not just of charts and maps, but a system through which they could understand and employ the heavenly bodies in their various mundane and 'spiritual' efforts.

These early scientists observed events in Nature-at-large and within their personal lives, and correlated those events, changes, and circumstances that seemed to flow from or be influenced by the arrangement and placement of the heavens. They studied the cyclic nature of the heavenly progressions and the periodicity of the movements of the 'wanderers,' the Greek word from which the term 'planet' arises. These early scientists' philosophy of the Natural Sciences was then gradually taught and applied in one way or another in universities throughout the Mediterranean and Western European countries, until at least the beginning of the 18th century.

As these scientists formed and fashioned their astronomical knowledge, their philosophical inclinations were added to it, producing—among a vast number of other philosophical or occult and magical characteristics—an assignment of the planets to different hours or parts of the day and night, but in a certain order. Their occult and magical motivations were sparked not only from their observations of Nature and their own lives, but from their deeper philosophical apprehensions of the planets and the influences these planets produced upon all life. As a result, we have the planetary assignments to the hours of the day and night but in the special sequence mentioned.

These assignments were later commented upon and used by the author of the *Three Books*, and are still in use in today's magical systems. In our case, we calculate the times of sunrise and sunset as the beginning of that process by which the planets are then assigned to both twelve-hour periods of any given day. According to the sequence of these planets derived by the ancient astrologers and used by (later) magicians, we in turn ascribe them to these hours of the day and night. This is therefore the first step in the mechanical part of deriving the Kabbalistic periods under which ritual and ceremonial acts can successfully be performed. Now that you are aware of what we will be doing and why, the rest will flow easily.

Calculation of the Hours of the Day and Night Using the Agrippa System

The first information the reader will need for calculating the hours of the day and night are the exact times of sunrise and sunset for the geographical position where they live. Hence, the individual will need to know the exact longitude and latitude of his or her town or city, since no doubt that is where they will spend the great majority of their time, and consequently, the place in which they will be practicing their magic.

While there are many astrological books, magazines, and guides out there ready to provide this information for six dollars or so, I have never found them to be very precise. They wind up leaving it up to the individual to complete some tedious calculations which, although very simple from a mathematical point of view, are messy to work with, and which inevitably encourage calculation errors. You can save your money and obtain the most mathematically precise sunrise and sunset times by accessing any computer, logging onto the World Wide Web, and going to the following web address:

http://aa.usno.navy.mil/data/docs/RS_OneDay.html

When this address is placed into the URL Field (Universal Resource Locator field) of the web browser, it will take you to the United States Naval Observatory's web page of "Astronomical Applications Department—Complete Sun and Moon Data for One Day." On that page you will be able to enter the state or territory where you live, along with the actual city or town. After pressing the enter button on the web page, you will receive a display of the times of sunrise and sunset for your exact location for any day of the year. And surprise! It will also give you the exact latitude and longitude of your location as well, so you need not worry about obtaining this data from those six-dollar books in order to figure it out for yourself!

HOWEVER—*you can save yourself a lot of bother, and simply scroll down the web page to the Notes section. By doing so, in the third paragraph you will find an option for printing out **all** of the times of* *sunrise and sunset for your location for the entire year on one notebook size piece of paper.* Do this, and you are all set for an entire year of using the Agrippa System of Hours of the Day and Night.

Now, to find the length of each of the twelve hours of the day for any day of the year, simply calculate the number of minutes between sunrise and sunset. Divide this number by twelve, and the quotient is the number of minutes in each of the twelve hours of that day. Next, subtract this number from 120—the number of minutes in two hours—which will give you the number of minutes in each of the twelve hours of the night, that is, in each of the hours from sunset to sunrise. The rest of the hourly system chart construction is very simple and mechanical (see the tables of Figure 1 and Figure 2 at the end of this chapter), but as with anything new, can cause problems until you are familiar with it. To eliminate this possibility, let's take an example to make the point clear.

(Here I will use the example taken from my second book, *Kabbalistic Cycles and the Mastery of Life.*) I am writing this from my specific location on Wednesday, August 25, 2004. According to my latitude and longitude, the times of sunrise and sunset are 5:28 AM Standard Time and 6:51 PM Standard Time. (When obtaining the sunrise and sunset data from the web page, be certain to *always* specify that you want your chart in Standard Time for your location. Daylight Savings Time is not acceptable, since we need the true time to determine each period of the planetary influences.)

Simple calculations show that there are a total of eight-hundred and three (803) minutes between sunrise and sunset for my position in this country. Now let's proceed in a stepwise fashion, to make it easy to follow this simple procedure.

1. Divide the total time of the hours between sunrise and sunset by twelve. That is, [803 ÷ 12]. When you do, you will find this yields 66.9167 minutes for each of the twelve hours of the day. Do not round off just yet. You need to carry this accuracy of the calculation through so your hours of the day and night end when they should. This extreme accuracy is not some weird penchant of mine for precision. Rather, as in higher mathematics where the process of rounding off can seriously effect the results obtained in the final answer, that same logic applies here. Specifically, an error made at this point will grow in magnitude, because this initial

value error will become compounded as further calculations are carried out.

2. Now refer to Figure 2—the Kabbalistic Table of the Planetary Hours Ruling the Day(s) Specified—and record the data you have so far in a copy of the table given in Figure 2. (Figure 2 is a blank chart that you can enlarge and photocopy so you won't have to make a new one each time. Also notice that the actual example we are plotting out will be found in Figure 1, so please refer to it throughout this example.) On your chart, record the Name of the Day, the Date, the time of sunrise and sunset, and the division process that gave you the number of minutes in each of the twelve hours of the day. For me, in this example, today is Wednesday, August 25, 2004, 5:28 AM Standard Time, 6:51 PM Standard Time, [803 ÷ 12 = 66.9167] (day).

3. Next, subtract the number of minutes in each day hour from one-hundred and twenty to get the number of minutes for each hour of the night, and enter it into your chart. For me, this would be: [120 − 66.9167 = 53.0833] minutes for each night hour.

4. Label your chart for no more than three days at a time. In the example, you will see Wednesday through Friday, but we will follow through our example for Wednesday's calculation only, to be explained later. Now for the Key, which is a handy mnemonic device for remembering the order of the planets for those of you who are new to this idea. The Key is *"The first hour of the day of every day, takes the planet that rules that day."* The rulers of the days of the week are classically assigned as:

> Monday = ruled by the Moon = 9
> Tuesday = ruled by Mars = 5
> Wednesday = ruled by Mercury = 8
> Thursday = ruled by Jupiter = 4
> Friday = ruled by Venus = 7
> Saturday = ruled by Saturn = 3
> Sunday = ruled by Sun = 6

Thus, Mercury and its attributions and the matters it rules is the governing planet of this first hour of the day. As such, it provides for the effects and the matters it rules, during this hour. For practice, you can do as I have done and enter "Mer" in column one, row one—or cell 1—on a sample chart of your own.

And what is the mnemonic device for remembering the order of the planets? Easy! It's just "3, 4, 5, 6, 7, 8, 9, and back again!" You will see this applied in the next step.

5. Please look at the chart again. You will see that the left hand division, labeled "Hours of the Day" is divided into three columns for Wednesday through Friday in this example, and that each column is divided into twelve rows, making twelve cells, one for each of the twelve hours of the days, for Wednesday through Friday. The same holds true for the right hand division of the chart. There are three columns, each divided into twelve rows labeled "Hours of the Night," producing twelve cells, one for each of the twelve hours of the night for each of the three days listed on the chart.

So the question now becomes, "What do I put in the remaining eleven cells of the Hours of the Day, and what gets put into the twelve cells of the Hours of the Night for Wednesday, in this example?" Here is where the mnemonic comes into play. It's just, "3,4,5,6,7,8,9 and back again!" You have 'Mer' in the first row, first column (cell 1). And what number does Mercury take? 8, of course. So what happens now? Use the mnemonic! "3,4,5,6,7,8,9 and back again!" What comes after 8? As we know, it is Nine (9). So place a small 9 off to the side in the next cell directly beneath Mer (cell 2). Now you have the first two cells filled in.

To fill in the rest of the cells for the Hours of the Day, just, "3,4,5,6,7,8,9, and back again!" That is, start again at the number three (3), place it in the next or the third cell, and proceed to do the same with numbers 4,5,6,7,8, and 9. Now you will have nine of the twelve cells for the Hours of the Day for Wednesday filled in. That is, from the first hour of the day through the ninth. To fill in the final three cells and thus completing the twelve Hours of the Day of Wednesday, you simply "...and back again!" Start at number three (3), place this in the tenth cell, and the numbers four (4) and five (5) into the eleventh and twelfth cells, respectively. You're almost done.

Now look at the list above of the planets to which these numbers are assigned. See what I mean? Next to each number in each cell, you now simply write the names of the corresponding planets. In this case, all twelve cells will be filled in with—

Cell 1 — Mer(cury) = 8

Cell 2 — (the) Moon = 9
Cell 3 — Sat(urn) = 3
Cell 4 — Jup(iter) = 4
Cell 5 — Mars = 5
Cell 6 — (the) Sun = 6
Cell 7 — Venus = 7
Cell 8 — Mer(cury) = 8 (as the planets' sequence repeats)
Cell 9 — (the) Moon = 9
Cell 10 — Sat(urn) = 3
Cell 11 — Jup(iter) = 4
Cell 12 — Mars = 5

And there you are. All of the planetary attributions for the twelve Hours of the Day for Wednesday are completely and accurately filled in. What's next? Let's take care of the twelve Hours of the Night.

6. Look at the second division on the Kabbalistic Cycles Chart. It is labeled "Hours of the Night." Under the column labeled Wednesday, you have twelve empty cells. How do you fill them in? "3,4,5,6,7,8,9 and back again!" With what number did you end the twelfth hour of Wednesday? The number five (5) which is equal to the planet Mars. So, in the first cell of the Hours of the Night of Wednesday, you start again at the number six (6), and continue, 7,8,9. The first four cells are filled. As to the remaining eight cells? "…and back again!" The fifth cell will take the number three (3). In succession after that we have, 4,5,6,7,8,9, the last number of which will occupy the eleventh cell of the column. The twelfth cell is, of course, three (3) again.

By looking at the list of planets assigned to these numbers, you can write in their names or the abbreviations just as you did for the Hours of the Day. Take a look at the list again to see the Planet–Number designations. You now have the entire chart for all twelve Hours of the Day and Night for this particular Wednesday, filled in almost completely. Notice the twelve larger empty spaces (periods column) next to each of the cells in both divisions of the chart. Of course, you know the *times of the planetary rulers must be placed in them.* Otherwise, you would only know which planet rules each of the twelve Hours of the Day and each of the twelve Hours of the Night, but you would not know *when* those times of rule begin and end! That's the next and final part of this particular process.

7. Now is the time to break out your trusty, humdinger of a calculator. You will need it from here on in! In Step 1 you calculated there were 66.9167 minutes for each hour of the day in this particular example. Enter this number into your calculator's memory cell. (In Step 2, your calculation showed there were 53.0833 minutes for each hour of the night. Don't worry about this latter number right now.)

(I do not mean to be condescending or picayune in my approach and detailed explanation, but have written this out in this style in order to assist those readers who are unfamiliar with this or other astrologically-based hourly systems.)

Now, to fill in the times during which each of the planets rule, begin with the Hours of the Day division, and start with the first hour of the day in cell 1, ruled by Mer(cury). From the sunrise/sunset data you obtained from the United States Naval Observatory web page, you know the day begins at 5:28 AM Standard Time. Hence the planet Mercury begins its rule at that time. But when does it end, and the next hour ruled by the Moon begin? The minutes part of the hour is where we begin our calculation.

Since there are sixty (60) minutes in an hour, subtract *from* the 28 in your calculator window, 60, which will give you –32 minutes. That's *minus* 32 minutes. This is only by the calculator's convention, since you actually use a negative sixty (60) to add to your plus twenty-eight (28). It's of no consequence mathematically, I assure you. It is simply the technique employed here, and it is perfectly correct mathematically.

Of course, we can't do anything with a set of negative integers here, so we add the stored number in the memory cell to it. That is, $[-32 + 66.9167 = 34.9167]$ minutes. Obviously, since $[-32]$ took you to 6:00 AM, the remaining 34.9167 minutes is that part of the next hour—the hour of 6:00 AM—in which Mercury is still ruling. Hence, the time in which Mercury has its effect is from 5:28 AM ST–6:35 AM ST. Notice here—and only here—you can round off.

The rule of thumb to use in all rounding off procedures in this Cycles System is to look at the first number to the right of the decimal place: the "tenths" position. If it is five (5) or higher, round up to the next minute, as was done here. *If this number is five (5) or less, round down.* Let me make this point clear. For the sake of argument, say the final number was, "34.2167" In that case, the hour would have ranged from 5:28 AM ST to 6: 34 AM ST.

These small differences do make a significant difference, not simply in the calculations, but in using the system in daily life. Why? I wish I had a penny for each time something happened within the last minute or two of a given hour. If I did, I'd be a rich man right now! The moral is, don't introduce any more error into your life than is absolutely necessary. In this matter, it certainly isn't necessary at all.

Thus, in the space to the left of the first cell occupied by Mer(cury), you record, "5:28 AM ST–6:35 AM ST," the way I have illustrated in Figure 1.

Owing to some slight mathematical manipulations that you will run into when calculating your daily charts—and which could cause some confusion for you at first—it seems best if we finish the twelve Hours of the Day here, together, calculating the times when each planet is 'in effect' as it is referred to in occult and magical literature.

So let's move on to cell 2 directly beneath Mer(cury). Since Mercury's effect ends at 6:35 AM, that will be the exact minute the Moon's effect in cell 2 will begin. So please enter that into your chart so you can follow along in this example. The calculation for this is then: 34.9167—*the original number received from the finished Mercury hour calculation, and not the rounded off number*—minus 60 = -25.0833 (minutes). Add the number 66.9167 in the memory cell of your calculator to it, to yield 41.8333 (minutes). By the same reasoning we used for the first hour of the day where we sub-tracted sixty (60) minutes from 34.9167, and which took us up to the sixth hour of the morning, that same process here takes us up to the second hour, in which there are 41.8333 minutes remaining in that hour for the lunar effect to hold. Rounding off we get 41.8333 = 42 minutes. The length of the lunar hour is then from 6:35 to 7:42 AM ST.

For the third hour of the day, ruled by Sat(urn) on the chart: we begin with the *precise* final number received for the ending of the lunar hour, which was 41.8333. Now: [41.8333 - 60 = -18.1667 + 66.9167 = 48.7500], or 8:49 AM. So record 7:42 to 8:49 AM in your sample chart.

The fourth cell, occupied by Jupiter is calculated in exactly the same way as the first three. That is: [48.7500 - 60 = -11.2500 +

66.9167 = 55.6667] minutes or, rounded off, 56. Thus the time in which the Jupiter influence rules is from 8:49 to 9:56 AM ST.

Using the same procedure for the fifth period: [55.6667 - 60 = -4.3333]. But when we add + 66.9167 to it, we receive 62.5834, clearly, over the sixty-minutes in any given hour. Why? Because we are working with a fixed limit of a sixty-minute period in an hour, true for calculations of the planetary hours for the day and night of *any* system. To offset this problem, you simply pay attention to the number that results when you subtract sixty (60). If that number—when added to the negative figure received from the subtraction—yields a number over sixty, you must subtract another sixty (60) minutes from the time-figure received, to bring the final result under the sixty-minute limit.

It is not hard at all. Just by inspection, you will be able to determine if the number received from the subtraction will give a new number greater than sixty, that is, when the number in your memory cell is added to it. It works like this: to find the time of the fifth hour of the day in the example, proceed as follows: [55.6667 - 60 = -4.3333]. Subtract another 60 as instructed: [-4.333 (-60) = -64.333]. To this figure, add the number in your calculator's memory cell—the length of each hour of the day, 66.9167 (minutes). This now yields: [-64.333 + 66.9167 = 2.5834] which is rounded off to 3. Since you began this fifth hour at 9:56 AM ST, and passed through one complete sixty (60) minute period through your calculations, you also passed through the 10 o'clock hour and entered the eleventh hour. Since you began this fifth hour at 9:56 AM ST, and have three (3) minutes remaining, you are now three minutes into the eleventh hour. This now gives you the time during which Mars—the ruler of this fifth hour of Wednesday—has dominion: 9:56 to 11:03 AM ST. Without further comment, let's work through the remaining seven periods of the Hours of the Day in this example.

Sixth Hour of the Day: [2.5834 - 60 = -57.4167 + 66.9167 = 9.5000]. Sixth hour period: 11:03 to 12:10 PM.

Seventh Hour of the Day: [9.5000 - 60 = - 50.5000 + 66.9167 = 16.4167]. Seventh hour period: 12:10 to 1:16 PM.

Eighth Hour of the Day: [16.4167 - 60 = - 43.5833 + 66.9167 = 23.3333]. Eighth hour period: 1:16 PM ST to 2:23 PM ST.

Ninth Hour of the Day: [23.3333 − 60 = −36.6667 + 66.9167 = 30.2500]. Ninth hour period: 2:23 to 3:30 PM.

Tenth Hour of the Day: [30.2500 − 60 = −29.7500 + 66.9167 = 37.1667]. Tenth hour period: 3:30 to 4:37 PM.

Eleventh Hour of the Day: [37.1667 − 60 = −22.8333 + 66.9167 = 44.0833]. Tenth hour period: 4:37 to 5:44 PM.

Twelfth Hour of the Day: [44.0833 − 60 = −15.9167 + 66.9167 = 51.0000]. Tenth hour period: 5:44 to 6:51 PM ST.

As you can see, the twelfth hour of the day ended on the exact minute at which sunset began, according to the Naval Observatory's data; a check on your work that confirms your calculations are correct to this point. This is also the start time of the first hour of the night, which we will now examine in some lesser but sufficient detail.

Move over to the second division on your chart—the one on the right side of the paper—labeled, Hours of the Night. Of course, you have all the planets ruling each hour already recorded in the twelve cells, and now simply need to figure out the times when each of those planets begins and ends its rule. As I mentioned, the hour and minute when sunset occurs—in this case 6:51 PM ST—constitutes the hour and minute when the first hour of the night also begins. So please add 6:51 PM (ST) to cell 1 of Wednesday as the start-time for the first Hour of the Night of Wednesday.

Since you converted the numbers in your chart into their planetary correspondences earlier, you should see Sun in cell 1. To calculate the time of the Sun's influence, recall that the lengths of the Hours of the Day and Night differ, and will throughout the year, except for the dates on which the Vernal (spring) and Autumnal Equinoxes occur. Since you know there are 66.9167 minutes in a day hour, and you previously subtracted this number from 120, you also know you have 53.0833 minutes in each of the hours of the night for this day, and that this is the figure you will be using to fill in the times in which the planets ruling the hours of the night have effect.

Since I have run through an entire series of calculations with you in calculating the times for the Hours of the Day in this example, it would be excessively redundant to belabor the process you now have firmly in hand. This being the case, we will work through the calculations for the first two hours of the night, and let you fill in the remaining ten. *Remember, in order for your calcula-tions to be correct, you will also have a check here to rely upon: and that is, that the twelfth Hour of the Night in this example will end precisely on the minute the Day Hours began—5:28 AM ST—thus completing one complete day.* So let's do those first two calculations to get you started.

First Hour of the Night: [51.0000 (the exact figure for the time the twelfth hour of the day ended) minus 60 = –9.0000 + 53.0833 = 44.0833]. The time period in which the Sun rules this first hour of the night is therefore, 6:51 PM ST to 7:44 PM ST.

The second hour of the night, the hour ruled by Venus as you can see from your chart, is: [44.0833 – 60 = –15.9167 + 53.0833 = 37.1666.] Rounded off by our rule of thumb, we have the time period during which Venus rules as 7:44 to 8:37 PM.

We will mention only one more cell. For cell 8, Sun, the exact start minute is 2.5831. When our memory cell figure of 53.0833 is added to this figure, we would still be under sixty minutes. There-fore, in this case, it is not necessary to subtract sixty minutes from the exact start time. However, if you do not notice this when you first do your calculation, and you find you have a final end time that is a minus figure, you can just add sixty minutes back again.

The remaining ten hours are calculated in exactly the same way, and will end at exactly at 5:28 AM ST, the exact minute of sunrise of the day being calculated. You are finished. You not only know the sequence of the planetary rulers for this day, but the exact times during which each of them rules both the Hours of the Day and the Hours of the Night.

A few word of working advice about your daily use of these calculations:

When making your charts, it is perfectly permissible to do the calculations for one day, and to use those same calculations for an additional two consecutive days. For instance, the times of sunrise to sunset and sunset to sunrise used in the Wednesday example above, can be safely extended into Thursday and Friday. Conse-quently, you will have a chart with only one set of times for the Hours of the Day and Night, but three days worth of planetary rulers. Why can you use one set of times for up to three days? There are two reasons:

1. The precision of your calculations ensures that although the times of sunrise to sunset and sunset to sunrise most certainly change everyday, those changes over any following two consecutive twenty-four hour periods will usually be fairly negligible due to the precision of those calculations. This means that after rounding off, the times over a three-day period will show such slight variation, that other variables such as the clock or watch you use to set the chart up in the first place cannot have such precision to enable you to obtain the 'exact' time each and every time. You would need an atomic clock for that!

2. Except at those times of the year when the length of the days and nights change rapidly, such as the first few weeks after either the Summer and Winter Solstice or the Vernal and Autumnal Equinox, the changes in the actual fractions of a second between the times of (up to) three successive days and nights over a given twenty-four hour period are very negligible. When the times do change rapidly as noted above, I recommend doing a chart for no more than two days at a time. That is, one set of sunrise/sunset and sunset/sunrise times for two days instead of for three. Frankly, this is only marginally necessary.

A further word of counsel might be of benefit to the reader at this point. As I explained earlier, in my opinion—based upon my use of the Agrippa System of Hours of the Day and Night almost exclusively for over forty years—this system is easier to use than any other, in addition to it proving to be extremely effective. *However*—and there is always a catch in everything as the reader knows—this system must be used *knowledgeably*. What do I mean by this? *Time your daily ritual performances according to the nature of your work.*

For example, if you are going to practice the Lesser Banishing Ritual of the Pentagram as it is classically given, you will most certainly be banishing from the angle of Earth, as you know. Therefore, the most beneficial times to practice on any given day will be during those hours which have the correspondence of the Element Earth: Venus and Saturn. Of course, from your calculations of the hours of the day and night, the times when these two 'Earth Planets' rule will change with each day. Or you may decide to perform the Lesser Invoking Ritual of the Pentagram to invoke the Element Fire, in which case, you would work under hours ruled by Mars and the Sun.

Never mind all other considerations for practicing. *When the appropriate planet rules, that is when you practice. Learn to use the Kabbalistic forces to your advantage!* Move *with* their flow, not against them! No doubt, the reader has heard that oft spouted New Age 'wisdom' to practice your ritual work at the same time each day! The warning goes on to say that this will get you into the habit of performing your rituals daily, and that if you don't perform them at the same time each day, you will feel a nagging, admonishing you to do your holy work!

First off, you are not doing some mundane task, the likes of which does fall into the category of such advice. When applied to mundane work such as studying or exercising, this approach will most certainly work, because it creates a psychological prompting that will nag at you until you do what you are *obligated* to do. But in magic, we are not concerned with psychological promptings anymore than we are with the opinions of the herd in this society, who condemn us for choosing this Path.

If you have to concern yourself with being prompted to do your daily magical work; if you have to be made to feel ill at ease by using this psychological device to better yourself and further your own life and evolution, then you don't belong in magic in the first place. Face up to it, and direct your energy into some other activity that will at least give you the fighting chance the herd is always telling you is your 'right' under this 'democratic' form of government. A callous opinion? Absolutely. But it is also a just one. A.E. Waite once said, "The true magician is brought forth from his mother's womb." He was right, and no amount of playing at magic or using cute little tricks to get you to do the Work that is yours to do, will displace the sentiments expressed in his words of wisdom. *Learn* and then *Work*, and *Work CORRECTLY!*

There is one final point I would like to address before ending this chapter. Note well that when you use the Agrippa System of Hours of the Day and Night to time your ritual practices, you will find that the effects produced under corresponding elemental but different planetary influences are very different. For example. If you perform the classical Lesser Banishing Ritual of the Pentagram by banishing from the Earth angle during a Venus hour, and then perform the same ritual during a Saturn hour, not only will the altered states of consciousness you achieve during these ritual performances be vastly different, but your normal daily consciousness after the practice of each will be markedly different as well.

In addition, the curious methods by which the forces summoned will act in order to change your external world of reality, will also be quite dramatically dissimilar. Such are the planetary—and hence Kabbalistic—effects of performing the same rite under different planetary influences. Be guided by your own perceptions and intuition and by the Kabbalistic forces that are now at your conscious, willful, beck and call.

Wednesday, August 25 through Friday, August 27, 2004
5:28 am Std, 6:51 pm, Std; 803 ÷ 12 = 66.9167 (day) and 53.0833 (night)

Hours of the Day

WED	THURS	FRI	PERIODS
8 Mer	4 Jup	7 Venus	5:28-6:35 am
9 Moon	5 Mars	8 Mer	6:35-7:42 am
3 Sat	6 Sun	9 Moon	7:42-8:49 am
4 Jup	7 Venus	3 Sat	8:49-9:56 am
5 Mars	8 Mer	4 Jup	9:56-11:03 am
6 Sun	9 Moon	5 Mars	11:03-12:10 pm
7 Venus	3 Sat	6 Sun	12:10-1:16 pm
8 Mer	4 Jup	7 Venus	1:16-2:23 pm
9 Moon	5 Mars	8 Mer	2:23-3:30 pm
3 Sat	6 Sun	9 Moon	3:30-4:37 pm
4 Jup	7 Venus	3 Sat	4:37-5:44 pm
5 Mars	8 Mer	4 Jup	5:44-6:51 pm

Hours of the Night

WED	THURS	FRI	PERIODS
6 Sun	9 Moon	5 Mars	6:51-7:44 pm
7 Venus	3 Sat	6 Sun	7:44-8:37 pm
8 Mer	4 Jup	7 Venus	8:37-9:30 pm
9 Moon	5 Mars	8 Mer	9:30-10:23 pm
3 Sat	6 Sun	9 Moon	10:23-11:16 pm
4 Jup	7 Venus	3 Sat	11:16-12:09 am
5 Mars	8 Mer	4 Jup	12:09-1:03 am
6 Sun	9 Moon	5 Mars	1:03-1:56 am
7 Venus	3 Sat	6 Sun	1:56-2:49 am
8 Mer	4 Jup	7 Venus	2:49-3:42 am
9 Moon	5 Mars	8 Mer	3:42-4:35 am
3 Sat	6 Sun	9 Moon	4:35-5:28 am

Figure 1.
Kabbalistic Table of the Planetary Hours
Ruling the Days Specified

Hours of the Day				Hours of the Night			
			PERIODS				PERIODS

Figure 2.
Sample blank table for plotting the Kabbalistic Planetary Forces

Chapter Four

Concerning the Kabbalistic Knowledge Necessary for Effective Magical Practice

Preliminary Remarks

What is presented in this chapter and those that follow, are the essential Kabbalistic tenets (the hard data I spoke of earlier) from which you, the reader, will derive the knowledge—at first through your reasoning ability and later, through your intuitive faculty—that will enable you to call down the Kabbalistic forces needed for your magic to work *all of the time*. This chapter also addresses the importance of building and strengthening your subconscious state of subjective synthesis, and will move you along many fronts you may not have previously encountered, both Kabbalistic and magical.

Heed these readings well. Study them carefully. Understand them. Contemplate them until you apprehend them. Then, apply them to the Kabbalistic Analyses of your daily ritual work and greater, more important ceremonial work. To the extent that you do this, I tell you now, your magic will succeed as it has never succeeded before. You purchased this book for a purpose. I wrote it to help you along this hard, complex, highly dangerous, and difficult Path of Magic that you have chosen to travel. *Together*, we *will* make all the difference in your life.

As to the reader's subjective state. It is not simply his or her state of subjective synthesis that will determine how accurately the Kabbalistic forces will work, as important as this state is. The *conscious* knowledge of the Kabbalah—which includes its history, structure, the operational characteristics of its practical components, i.e., the Sephiroth, Paths, and their attributions—will likewise have an equal and direct bearing upon the accuracy and type of rational and intuitive insights the individual will derive from the willful use of the Kabbalah.

In this latter regard, put simply, the more the reader knows of these matters, not only will his or her subjective state be more stable and complete; but he or she will possess more practical knowledge upon which they can consciously draw in order to make an immediate and accurate interpretation of the Kabbalistic influences that lie behind any given ritual or ceremonial performance. In order to provide the reader with a comprehensive overview of the Kabbalah (also spelled Kabalah, Qabalah, and Cabala, depending upon the occult text or subject in which it is discussed), this chapter will be devoted to presenting an extensive discussion of what I consider to be *Classical Kabbalah*.

Owing to my feelings regarding the New Age and its schizophrenic, quick-fix, instant gratification mentality toward occult subjects, I will have nothing to do with a patchwork approach to this all important subject as is typically found in many current 'Kabbalah for Dummies' books available today. My other reason for presenting what I consider to be Classical Kabbalah, is that throughout my past forty-plus years in the occult in general and magic in particular, I have found that nearly all of my students became much more easily attuned, if you will, to the more rigorous approach to the Kabbalah, provided they started with the classical presentation of the subject immediately.

Indeed, other students who came to me with somewhat of a background in New Age Qabalah—as the New Age prophets denote the subject—found that they actually preferred the classical approach as I taught it. The reason for this is that they found it easier to integrate the disconnected bits and pieces of Kabbalistic thought using this classical approach. In short, and after some readjustment, these individuals found the classical approach to be more effortless than those New Age Qabalistic doctrines which treated the subject incompletely or mistreated it altogether.

Since it is my intent to get readers started now on building their state of subjective synthesis, while also laying a solid, conscious foundation of Kabbalistic knowledge, I strongly suggest that this chapter and those that follow be *very carefully studied*. If the reader will do this, he or she will be well on their way to achieving these ends. They may even come to realize that the Kabbalah is not as confusing, boring, or impossibly nebulous as many bemoan the New Age version of it to be. The few additional books mentioned along the way are highly recommended. One should *carefully* consider **expanding** their study of Classical Kabbalah through the study of these other resources, but only *after* a foundation has been laid through what is presented here.

For it must be remembered that regardless of the connectivity and depth of the Kabbalistic issues covered, it is not possible to present the complete Kabbalah in a single book. Even those individual text efforts that are dedicated to such an attempt fail, as the reader may already be aware. There are far too many facets of the Kabbalah to render its full presentation in a single volume. It will take an assiduous study of several of the recommended books to be cited here, over time, for the individual to ferret out the priceless gems of knowledge that are contained within the Heart of Kabbalah.

As such, these recommendations are provided as resource musts. Hence, by studying and contemplating them, the individual will continue to deepen his or her understanding of this incredibly important subject. In turn, these further explorations of Kabbalah will expand the reader's conscious understanding and subconscious comprehension and apprehension of the subject, giving rise to one of the most powerful, practical life tools imaginable.

The Classical Kabbalah—An Overview

I prefer to think of the Kabbalah as both a Hebrew and a Jewish system of theosophy. 'Hebrew' signifying that Mediterranean race of Semitic people, and 'Jewish' referring to the religious train of thought practiced primarily by such people. The term theosophy, however, is not used here in the common sense. Rather, for our purposes, it denotes a structured, unified belief system that encompasses Creation, the Universe, and the World as we know it, all of which is based upon mystical insights and Divine Revelations.

As to the word Kabbalah itself, it specifically refers to a collection of religious writings or doctrines received through tradition. However, it was not until around circa 1200 C.E. that the term

Kabbalah designated this complete, self-contained system of theosophy. In my opinion, the Kabbalah can be called a doctrine of Jewish Occultism, the bedrock of which is founded upon Hebrew Mysticism. There is a difference here, and it would do the reader well to further contemplate this subtlety.

From a historical perspective, the main canons employed to create the Kabbalah were the *Zohar*, or the *Book of Splendor*, a large tome of books dealing with mysticism, and the *Sepher Yetzirah*, or the *Book of Formation*, which is actually a synthesis of medieval mysticism and scientific thought. The date of origin of this latter work has been contested for millennium, but from all historical accounts, it seems to have originated before 800 C.E.

More legendary views hold that one rabbi by the name of Simeon bar Yochai, along with his son, hid from the Romans in a cave for thirteen years. Being highly learned in the mysticism of their people, the rabbi and his son produced both the *Zohar* and the *Sepher Yetzirah* during that thirteen-year period of seclusion. It is said the books were written by them around circa 100 C.E., and that the content of the *Zohar* is actually a written account of the dialogues that took place between God and Adam, while Adam was still in paradise. Most modern authorities however, hold to the view that the *Zohar*, which was popularized around 1200 C.E. by one Moses de Leon, was actually authored by him.

Even so, it contains an enormous number of important and ancient mystical insights, speculations, and wisdom traditions of the Hebrew people. The *Zohar*, a rather substantial collection of writing, is actually a set of commentaries on another important Hebrew text, the *Pentateuch*. The *Zohar* includes eleven dissertations on the *Pentateuch*, of which the *Secret of Secrets*, the *Book of Secrets*, the *Mysteries of the Pentateuch*, and the *Hidden Interpretation* are believed by many to be the most important of those writings.

As a system of theosophy, the Kabbalah deals with the nature of God, the ten spheres of divine emanations radiating from God (which are referred to as Sephiroth in a plural sense, and as Sephirah when speaking of a single sphere or divine emanation), along with the natures of angelic beings, man, and the worlds or aspects of the Intelligible and the Sensible, as these latter relate to the Sephirothal concepts.

While the concepts of Intelligible and Sensible are considered by some to be advanced Kabbalistic concepts, I view them as properly belonging to the more rigorous Classical Kabbalah. I have presented them here and have tried to integrate them in such a way as to lend a more rounded, extensive explanation of the subject. While most of the discussion that follows in this section has been drawn from Classical Kabbalah directly, other parts were derived from my own mystical and meditative introspections, and from personal experimental work in the fields of Kabbalah, Magic, and the Occult in general.

By creating a synthesis of these intellectual, mystical, and occult experiences, it is my intention to help the reader further their own understanding of this fascinating and practical theosophy in a more holistic manner, while not compromising the essential tenets of the Classical Kabbalah. You will discover I have used sufficient repetition, both in different ways and in different places, as a learning aid.

The ten divine emanations, *through* their Intelligible and Sensible manifestations in both concept and form respectively, are represented by a geometrical figure of ten circles or spheres, connected to each other in a precise pattern of twenty-two lines or Paths, as Figure 3 illustrates. These paths represent the specific relation that any two or more spheres so connected bear to each other. They represent the particular interconnectedness that exists between the attributes, correspondences, and concepts that those spheres or Sephiroth represent in both the Intelligible and Sensible worlds.

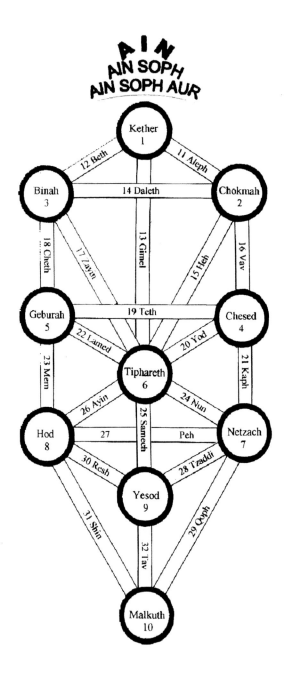

Figure 3. The Tree of Life.

Now, the Intelligible world can be thought of as the realm of pure abstraction of a specific attribute manifested by God, or a particular behavior in which God involves Itself. The very idea of the pure abstraction of a concept or behavior enables the higher aspect of that attribute or behavior to become comprehensible to the limited mentality of the human mind. Put another way, by understanding that some abstraction exists behind the normal or casual meaning of a concept, the individual realizes there is some ethereal aspect of that attribute or behavior implied, beyond which the concept is taken to mean in the everyday world of humankind. Hence the meaning behind the term Intelligible.

The manifestations of attributes or properties of God are ten in number, and exist as Intelligible, pure abstractions of particular aspects of God, which are brought down into conceptual form for mankind's understanding through Divine Revelation and the Mystical Experience of Union with the Divine. These abstractions are rendered more comprehensible and actually manifest in Creation *through* the 'Sensible' nature of each Sephirah, and through the twenty-two interconnecting Paths.

In the Kabbalistic context, the idea of Sensible refers to the manifestations and laws of Nature, and the methods by which Nature brings about form in the physical world. But also in Kabbalistic terms, the idea of Sensible moves beyond this. It also designates those ideas, perceptions, mental constructs, activities, and actions, by which we as humankind superficially react, act, and interact with Nature. It can be Nature 'out there,' as, for instance, in our passing appreciation of a breathtaking sunset, or within our own minds, when we struggle to understand something about the workings of Nature 'out there,' or of our own human nature.

In a way, the Sensible can be thought of as a kind of Divine superficiality brought down to earth. It forms our universe, all aspects of Nature—along with the laws of Nature as they operate—both *within* and *without* our bodies and *everyday* minds. By contrast, our divine inheritance as Creations of God, enables us to reach up through our daily nature and through mystical, meditative, or magical techniques, extend ourselves upward, and share some aspect of the Intelligible by comprehending, understanding, and finally apprehending something that cannot easily be formed into words, but only experienced in silence.

As an example. The causal appreciation of that magnificent sunset can be transformed from a Sensible *event* into a transcendent Intelligible *experience* if—through some technique—the beauty and grandeur of that sunset effects us at all levels of our complex existence, and produces something more within us. This would be something we *experience*, but cannot easily express in words.

While this may appear to be doubletalk or confusing at first, if the reader will take a line at a time and think through these perhaps unfamiliar terms and ideas, he or she will readily grasp the basics. Remember. When attempting to put that which is transcendent into words, difficulties must, by definition, arise. Why? Because when the reader contemplates these words of explanation, a transition is being attempted to move from the Sensible to the Intelligible itself. But once that transition is achieved, it becomes a matter of course for the reader to continue the process, building or adding to his or her Kabbalistic knowledge foundation, depending upon previous familiarity with the subject. In the process, the individual's state of subjective synthesis becomes so enhanced, that their results stemming from the use of the Kabbalah skyrocket.

In Classical Kabbalah, three fundamental ideas are considered first. They are referred to as the **Three Veils of the Unmanifest**, namely, the **Ain**, the **Ain Soph**, and the **Ain Soph Aur**. The Ain—the Nothingness—is the Causeless Cause of all causes. It simply was and is. It is not a being. It is not even a Nothing, but rather, it is *No-Thing*. As the *Zohar* explains, "Before having created any shape in the world, before having produced any form, HE was alone, without form, resembling nothing. Who could comprehend HIM, as HE then was, before creation, since HE had no form?" HE is that which is incomprehensible and unknowable, and as such, HE does not exist.

But this Unknowable, conceived of IT–SELF as the AIN Soph—Infinity—in order to be comprehensible to ITSELF. It then became the Ain Soph Aur, or Absolute Boundless Light, a limitless Existence-Ideation. (Here, the concept of Ideation is taken to mean something that is imagined in the mind. A mind-construct with or without plan, according to the impulses of the Ideationist.) It contains the entire universe, while yet pervading every part of it.

This Existence-Ideation also includes all that is manifest and unmanifest, including all forms of light, energy, matter, space, time, mind, being, etc. IT is so boundless, and ITS nature so unknown, that the mind of man cannot conceive of IT, any more than it can of the Ain Soph, which is Infinity itself. Because IT not only contains all of that which has been made manifest, and in principle also contains that which at any moment is as yet unmanifest, in a certain mystical sense, this IT is also nonexistent.

In the process of apprehending ITS own Existence-Ideation, (here, to apprehend means to become conscious of; to understand through a profundity not within normal perceptual definition and experience), this IT—this Ain Soph Aur—became alive and creative in order to give meaning to, and to project that meaning of ITS existence. IT did this is in a dynamic sense, by projecting the ten Sephiroth—also referred to as 'Intelligences' in Kabbalistic literature—through which IT could express its dynamism into the world of the unmanifest (non-form) and the manifest (the world of form).

From the root No-Thing, the Ain, the Nothingness, and through its progressions, the Glyph of the Tree of Life sprang into form, a symbolic model of the forms, forces, life, and ideation of the One Existence-Ideation. The Glyph became the medium through which God *as* the Existence-Ideation, or the IT, was able to become active, reactive, and create within its own Creation. The IT could only produce and project that which was and is of its own nature.

ITS first manifestation was as the Kether, the primal root source from which all issues and from which all will issue in the Intelligible and Sensible worlds. All must spring from it. It is indivisible and without dimension, yet it gives rise to all. It is the essential point of generation of all physical things, as well as the point of origin of all consciousness.

Kether, in all of its correspondences and concepts, represents and is itself all unification, and all indivisibility. It is ever in motion. It is the core of all life, and the metaphysical focus of all spiritual energy and beings. Mankind's Sensible perception of this first Sephirah has been made into the concept of the God of the physical universe, or the representation of that desire the IT had to become manifest. As ITS Nature was apprehended completely unto itself both before, during, and after assuming the form of the

Crown, it contained within it the other nine Sephiroth or Intelligences of the Tree of Life, each of which emanates from the previous one.

In other words, the second Sephirah proceeded from the first, the third from the second, the fourth from the third and so on, throughout the entire number sequence until the final expression was achieved in the tenth sphere, Malkuth. The Kabbalistic names of each, beginning at the top of the Glyph and following down in descending order are: Kether (the Crown; The Father), Chokmah (Wisdom; The Son), Binah (Understanding; The Mother), Chesed (Mercy), Geburah (Severity), Tiphareth (Beauty), Netzach (Victory), Hod (Glory), Yesod (Foundation), and Malkuth (Kingdom; the world of matter, the world of form).

It must be remembered that these are the pure abstractions or Intelligible concepts. They are the purest forms of attributes which flow from God. The more mundane forms, the Sensible qualities that mankind can understand, are the stepped-down qualities that have their roots in each of these pure abstractions.

Another fundamental attribute assigned to the Sephiroth of the basic Tree of Life glyph are numerical correspondences. That is, Kether = One (1), Chokmah = Two (2), Binah = Three (3), Chesed = Four (4), Geburah = Five (5), Tiphareth = Six (6), Netzach = Seven (7), Hod = Eight (8), Yesod = Nine (9), and Malkuth = Ten (10). Beyond Kether, in emptiness or beyond or above—as the student may wish to imagine them in order to comprehend in human terms the structural arrangement of the Tree and its point of origin—exists the lowest of the Three Veils of the Unmanifest that were mentioned earlier.

That is, the Ain Soph Aur, the first of the Three Veils, followed by the Ain Soph, which is the second of the Three Veils and which can be thought of as being behind or above the Ain Soph Aur, and finally at some remote, non-conceptual point beyond or above the Ain Soph, the third and highest of the Three Veils, the Ain. In the case of Ain, its numerical correspondence is zero (0). Please refer to Figure 3 for a graphical representation of these Three Veils of the Unmanifest.

Owing to the individual Intelligible and Sensible natures of the ten Sephiroth, the Kabbalah postulates them as existing within four planes or Four Worlds of being. Atziluth is the highest of the Worlds, and through its Intelligible nature, it corresponds to the realm of Divine Being. As that abstraction of the Intelligible which mankind can comprehend, it is said to correspond with the ideas of Jung's Archetypal World.

The next lower world is Briah, or the World of Creation, followed by Yetzirah, the World of Formation. The Worlds are said to end in Assiah, the World of Matter. There are two methods by which Kabbalists schematically represent the placement of the Four Worlds on the Tree of Life. I refer to them as the overt method of placement and the occult method of placement.

In the occult method of placement, the *Zohar* assigns an entire tree of ten Sephiroth to each of the Four Worlds of the Kabbalah. This placement is extremely important from a theoretical and theosophical point of view, but becomes rather complex, at least as far as working out the preliminary pattern is concerned. As such, it is beyond the scope of this book. The overt method of placement is much simpler, and may serve better for a graphical comprehension of the Four Worlds.

In this method, Kether is the sole Sephirah that occupies the World of Atziluth. It is the root of all, and projects the other nine Sephiroth from itself, with Atziluth being the divine or archetypal realm of being in which Kether exists. The next World, Briah, the Creative World, is occupied by Chokmah and Binah. In Briah, we have the realm of pure idea and universal potency or force, energizing all. As Atziluth is the realm of pure being or divinity, Briah is the plane of the archangelic beings, into whose hands the ceaseless ordering of the patterns underlying Creation have been entrusted.

Yetzirah—the World of Formation—consists of the Sephiroth Chesed, Geburah, Tiphareth, Netzach, Hod, and Yesod. That is, Sephiroth numbers Four (4) through Nine (9). It is the World of rarefied matter and energy, of force and form, electric, manifesting in various subtle levels. It is the region in which the tenuous states of rarefied energy and matter constantly transition back and forth between one another.

This is the angelic world of existence, whose governance is always in accord with the laws operating at this plane of Creation. All are coalesced in the lowest of the Four Worlds, the World of Assiah, the world of physical form, and the energy that underlies the gross expression of this three-dimensional form. In short, Assiah is the material world within which we live and move on a daily basis, and in which we have our normal sensory or conscious awareness.

It is within this fold of the Kabbalistic Tree of Life, with its Four Worlds and the Three Veils of the Unmanifest that the practical Kabbalist, the Mystic, and the Magician work. But for our more intensely practical application—while realizing that a theoretical knowledge of these features of the Kabbalah are also strictly necessary and must be obtained by the student over time—our concern will now focus on the more mundane characteristics of the Tree: the Sensible characteristics, forces, and attributions of the ten Sephiroth and the Twenty-Two Paths that interconnect them.

First, however, as promised, the list of musts that will help the reader attain this necessary theoretical knowledge of the Kabbalah. Remember, these readings will neither be fully understood nor comprehended by you in a conscious sense during a single reading, or even after many years of assiduous study. But as the root of all extends into Kether, so too will your labors and growing, conscious, understanding extend into the deepest recesses of your subjective mind. There, they will rapidly form a coherent, potent, energy-center of inner light and form that will influence you daily, permitting you to do so much more in your life. Yet even all of this will only be the beginning of the many blessings this inner comprehension will bestow upon you.

(While complete publication details of each of the following can be found in the Reference List at the end of this book, I have added a commentary to each one here, in order to help the reader through the seeming maze of available Kabbalistic literature. It would also be a good idea to begin to acquire these books at this juncture.)

A Garden of Pomegranates,[14] by Israel Regardie, offers a comprehensive view of the Kabbalah. It cites correspondences, attributes, and meanings of the components of the Tree from many different perspectives, thereby lending the new student insight into the importance and application of the Kabbalah. For the seasoned student, it will serve as an excellent refresher, while perhaps throwing new light on old concepts.

The Essential Kabbalah—The Heart of Jewish Mysticism,[15] by Daniel C. Matt, is an extraordinary book, giving an accurate and precise overview of the main tenets of Kabbalah. It should be studied in concert with Regardie's book.

Following this, Dion Fortune's *The Mystical Qabalah*,[16] should be carefully read and compared with Regardie's text. Despite New Age claims as to it being a dated approach, all of the material it presents is accurate—with but one issue I take strong exception to, and which is discussed later on. Her work is clear, and thoroughly presented within a well-designed framework.

Sefer Yetzirah, The Book of Creation,[17] by Aryeh Kaplan could be studied with profit. It sheds a great deal of light on the mystical as well as magical aspects of Kabbalah, and suggests that the text can be used to develop the individual's powers of concentration, telekinesis, and telepathy (notice these are psychic faculties, not the oft touted spiritual powers). It is unusual to say the least, but in my opinion it too is an extraordinarily valuable book.

Zohar, The Book of Splendor—Basic Readings from the Kabbalah,[18] edited by Gershom Scholem, is important for its peculiar insights into this ancient text. It could be studied after Regardie's, Matt's, Kaplan's, and Fortune's books.

De Arte Cabalistica. On the Art of the Kabbalah,[19] by Johann Reuchlin, is one of the most important texts on the subject that has ever been penned. Dating back to the 16th century, its knowledge is available today in a reprint edition. This text should be studied by itself, after the sequence of the former books has been gone through.

In the 19th century, the great Occultist, Eliphas Levi, wrote a three volume discourse on the mysteries of occultism. Of those three volumes, the first two are important for our purposes. Levi's first volume, *The Book of Splendours*,[20] and his second volume in the trilogy, *The Mysteries of the Qabalah*,[21] could be studied one at a time after completing Reuchlin's work.

Finally, there is the magnificent production, *The Holy Kabbalah*,[22] by Arthur Edward Waite. Despite the ranting of his intellectually deficient New Age detractors, the complexity of Waite's work—as opposed to his verbosity as his critics so love to label that complexity—is worth every bit of effort. His compound, shaded meanings within a single sentence; the structure of his rigor in presentation; his syntactical maneuvering—all leave no stone unturned in any of the occult subjects of which he wrote, and all make this the final text the diligent reader should study.

Throughout all of these readings, I also strongly recommend John Michael Greer's *The New Encyclopedia of the Occult*.[23] Its current day copyright does not betray its content, as so many of the current books in this genre do. It is extremely well structured, very complete, exceptionally accurate, and allows for ease of cross-referencing. Consider it your roadmap through the vast expanse of Kabbalistic literature. It will take time and hard mental effort, to be sure. But then, that's what Kabbalah—as with the rest of life—is all about.

The Sephiroth

In this section, we will lay the groundwork for those basic aspects of the Kabbalah as contained in the Tree of Life proper, that will eventually be built up into your subconscious state of subjective synthesis, and which you will use daily in your practical magical work. Each of the ten Sephiroth will be explored in this chapter. Both Intellectual and Sensible qualities and correspondences of each Sephirah will be given. As we progress through our exploration of the Kabbalah, the qualities and correspondences will be narrowed down into the Sensible characteristics and aspects exclusively. Where appropriate, a Commentary has been added to elucidate points that might be confusing, or which can pose problems later on when studying more advanced Kabbalistic literature.

In Chapter Five, we will discuss the twenty-two Paths of the Tree, while in Chapter Six we will add *the* fundamental correspondence traditionally assigned to the Paths: the Tarot attributions. But we will do more in that chapter as well. We will explore a new method of performing Path Working Magic that I have developed throughout the decades, and which many others have found to be quite effective when used as directed. And finally, in Chapter Seven, we will examine the practical magical and material associations ascribed to both the Sephiroth and their planetary attributions.

As the reader works through this material, his or her newly acquired knowledge of the Tree of Life will then be used to build up their Kabbalistic understanding in a step-by-step fashion. As in advanced mathematics, when we begin with postulates and proceed through a logical formalism, we eventually arrive at a specific method of solution for a *set* of problems being analyzed. In like manner, this approach applied to the Tree will illustrate the obvious nature of the Kabbalah itself. This system will then become apparent to the reader, never to be forgotten, lending itself to a direct and effective application in daily life.

Be aware that only a very limited number of attributions and qualities of the Sephiroth are given below. Yet this will be sufficient to get the magician up and running. The reader's study of the recommended texts will expand upon this list of attributions and qualities, along with a comprehension of the concepts. As the study of those other texts continues, the individual's understanding and apprehension will increase exponentially. Also, please remember I did not invent the attributions of the Sephiroth. They are general characteristics of the spheres, cited and distributed in one form or another throughout the voluminous recordings of occult, magical, mystical, and metaphysical literature.

Kether

Number on the Tree: One (1). *Primary Title*: Crown. *Other Titles*: the Inscrutable Monad; the Macroprosopus which according to the *Zohar* is The Great Countenance; in terms of the Christian trinity-theology and Neoplatonic cosmology from which the Christian idea of the Trinity was derived, Kether is the Father, or the First Existence; also The Ancient of Ancient; The Ancient of Days; The Head which is not; according to the *Sepher Yetzirah*, the Admirable of Hidden Intelligence; the Primordial Point. *Astrological Attribution*: the Primum Mobile, or that which is called the Beginnings of Turnings. *Intelligible Quality*: The First Cause; the Root of all things; the Initial Unity that was, is, and will be, and from which all else proceeds. *Peak Human Experience of this Sephirah*: Union with God. *Sensible Qualities*: As assigned by humankind for magical purposes, the God of the physical universe; the divine component, or the spark of divinity within the individual; the spiritual essence of the individual. *Color on the Tree*: white. *Color Scale*: In Atziluth, pure brilliance. In Briah, its color appears as a brilliant white. In Yetzirah, the pure brilliant white remains. In Assiah, the brilliant white becomes flecked with bright gold. *Elemental Attribution*: Air. *Polarity*: None. *Tarot Card Correspon-*

dence: the Four Aces of the Lesser Arcana, being one from each of the Four Suits.

Commentary: *The idea of polarity on the Tree can cause no small amount of confusion. First off, it must be remembered that the Sephiroth are states of existence, not physical points, positions, or stations. Neither do they occupy some portion of space 'out there' in the universe. Yet this 'polarity' is interpreted in human terms to be something with which the mind can identify. In this case, positive or negative, masculine or feminine, force or form.*

Since Kether is the "I AM" state of existence, it contains all potential, yet, as Dion Fortune states in her book, "The Mystical Qabalah," Kether...is pure being, all-potential, but not active...Wherever there is a state of pure, unconditioned being, without parts or activities, it is referred to Kether. But earlier I mentioned that Kether is ever in motion, so how can this be? In theological and theosophical fact, neither Fortune's comments nor mine contradict each other, owing to the state that Kether is in at any given moment, to use the human construct of time. In its pure state of potential, Kether is non-active. When its potential changes to a kinetic state, it becomes ever in motion.

In fact, the definitions that the science of physics gives to these two states is highly applicable here: potential, meaning the energy of position, that is, a placement or state without motion; and kinetic, meaning the energy of motion. In brief, while this Sephirah lacks polarity, yet it gives rise to the polarities of positive and negative, masculine and feminine, male and female, through its projections of the other nine Sephiroth. Such is a characteristic of its Intelligible and incomprehensible nature.

Chokmah

Number on the Tree: Two (2). *Primary Title*: Wisdom. *Other Titles*: In Christian trinity-theology and Neoplatonic cosmology, Chokmah is the Son. In Kabbalistic theosophy, the title of Father is assigned to this Sephirah; the Supernal Father; the Second Supernal. *Astrological Attribution*: the Zodiac. Chokmah is also assigned the planet Uranus as an attribution, but this is not typically used in Occult and Magical work. *Intelligible Quality*: that Divine Wisdom which is beyond human comprehension; the Illuminating Intelligence; that energetic, dynamic, all-conscious force underlying existence. *Peak Human Experience of this Sephirah*: the Vision of God. *Sensible Qualities*: Wisdom of the most subtle, profound type, of which humankind is capable of comprehending; the essential *impulse* behind the very essence of intellectualism; the Will that exists beyond one's personal, individual will, and which is the Divine Will within the individual. Magically, it is the 'True Will' of the aspirant: that part of the Will of God seeking to express itself in the world through the individual. It is also the Chiah, the energy of the eternal part of the Self. *Color on the Tree*: gray. *Color Scale*: In the World of Atziluth, Chokmah is an unadulterated, soft blue. In Briah, gray. In Yetzirah, a pearl gray that exhibits rainbow-like reflections. In Assiah, the color is a soft white, flecked with red, blue, and yellow. *Elemental Attribution*: Fire. *Polarity*: Chokmah is the primary positive, masculine, and active power of the Tree. It sits at the summit of what is called The Pillar of Mercy on the right side of the glyph of the Tree of Life. As such, it is the active dynamism of the Tree (but with the understanding given in the Commentary below). *Tarot Card Correspondence*: The Four Twos of the Lesser Arcana, being one from each of the Four Suits.

Commentary: The Four Twos of the Tarot's Lesser Arcana representing Chokmah, can indeed represent a dynamic force, positive and masculine in nature. But according to the Kabbalists, this is only true for Chokmah on the subtle planes of existence, owing to its being the second Sephirah of the three Supernals of the Supernal Triad of the Tree: Kether being the first Supernal, and Binah the third. When the Chokmah influence appears on the less subtle planes of form however, its force is negative. That is, it lends equilibrium to the world of form through it dual polarity–aspect.

Binah

Number on the Tree: Three (3). *Primary Title*: Understanding. *Other Titles*: The Great Mother; The Great Sea; The Universal Root Substance which our senses are in contact with, yet which is so rarefied we cannot perceive; the Sanctifying Intelligence. *Astrological Attribution*: The planet Saturn. *Intelligible Quality*: Divine Understanding, cognition of which mankind cannot perceive. *Peak Human Experience of this Sephirah*: the Summit of Sorrow, perceived as a universal experience. *Sensible Qualities*: The individualized, divine comprehending faculty within man, or the spiritual understanding of the Neshamah—one of the higher, spiritualized forces within the human soul; stability. On the more mundane level, owing to its planetary attribution of Saturn, issues relating to financial debts; the repayment of these debts; the acquisition of real estate; death; crops and agriculture; lassitude; inertia; lack of individual will; activities that require intensive thought followed by a period of consistent action; an influence that is good for legal matters in which justice is sought, and which involves the authorities: such as government offices, both state and federal, as well as police, judges, courts; also a good influence for bringing issues to the attention of those who have the power to decide an outcome favorable to the petitioner; excellent for literary work requiring deep insight; a positive period for attempting sales and the advancement of products through advertising by means of printed media; beginning or advancing any scientific pursuit; an excellent influence under which to engage in deep thought regarding any issue. This Saturanean influence however, is extremely adverse for seeking favors or recognition from those who can grant them. It is also adverse for: making investments, whether in the stock market or in any kind of business; beginning agricultural projects such as planting or seeding. It is also a very ill time for making new acquaintances, and is extremely adverse for beginning a marriage, the use of any medical remedy for body or mind, or attempting any cures of the body or mind by any metaphysical system. Additionally, it is very adverse for surgery of any kind, and a very unfortunate hourly influence under which to enter into a contract of any kind (see Commentary 1 below). *Color on the Tree*: black. *Color Scale*: In the World of Atziluth, a brooding crimson red. In Briah, a flat, all engulfing black. In Yetzirah, a dark, flat brown. In Assiah, a flat, cool gray, flecked with pink. *Elemental Attribution*: Water. *Polarity*: Binah is negative, feminine and passive, the essential feminine power of the Tree, just as Chokmah embodies the principle masculine power. Binah is situated at the summit of the Pillar of Severity on the glyph (see Commentary 2, below). *Tarot Card Correspondence*: The Four Queens of the Lesser Arcana, being one from each of the Four Suits.

Commentary 1: From Binah onward, the Sensible attributions of each Sephirah take on mundane qualities, in addition to their more aesthetic, humanly comprehensible characteristics. This is due to the nature of the planetary concepts themselves, of which the physical planets of the same name are simply projections in our physical universe. More will be said on this matter in the section dealing with the Paths of the Tree.

Commentary 2: On the subtle planes of existence, Binah is feminine, passive, and negative in polarity. Below these planes—in the world of form—she is positive, dynamic, and active. Why? Because 'she' is actually projected from Chokmah, and as such, represents 'his' masculine, positive, dynamic nature below the subtle planes—that is, in the world of form. It is through her dynamic aspect that the positive polarity of Chokmah is projected into the world of form, while the two together— both Chokmah and Binah—maintain equilibrium throughout the subtle planes and the planes of form. But Binah does not act simply as a mirror, projecting Chokmah's positive force below the Supernal Triad. In her feminine, passive nature, she provides equilibrium within the Chokmah-Binah dualism of the Supernal Triad in the World of Briah. Below this Triad, she projects the Chokmah, the positive principle in order to maintain equilibrium in the world of the other seven Sephiroth. As one cannot exist without the other, neither can one understand either of these two Sephiroth without considering its counterpart.

Chesed

Number on the Tree: Four (4). *Primary Title*: Mercy. *Other Titles*: Love; Majesty; Gedulah. According to the *Sepher Yetzirah,* also the "Receptacular Intelligence." Also, the Cohesive or Receptive Intelligence. *Astrological Attribution*: the planet Jupiter. *Intelligible Quality*: The Perfect Mercy and Love of God. *Peak Human Experience of this Sephirah*: the Vision of Love; the Experience of Supreme Mercy or Compassion stemming from that Vision of Love. *Sensible Qualities*: human love as a devotional force as it is applied to another person, an action, or objective; dedication stemming from love. On the mundane level, issues relating to or involving abundance; plenty; money; all aspects and types of growth and expansion; visions; dreams; spirituality as a way of life. This Jupiteranean influence is very good for beginning a new venture, a new plan, or a new idea of any kind, for working out the details of new plans and ideas, and for making contracts or agreements, regardless of their nature. It is an excellent influence under which to study and gain new knowledge, as it is for involving oneself in educational matters of any kind. It is a very fortunate influence under which to marry, and is a very beneficent period for making new acquaintances, borrowing money, and dealing with powerful or prominent people who can be of genuine benefit to your plans, ideas, and desires. It is likewise an excellent influence for purchasing or selling real estate, asking for favors from virtually anyone directly, and for indulging in all forms of speculation for profit. This influence also has a spontaneous, instinctive, and involuntary characteristic that must be guarded against, lest the individual becomes careless in weighing and analyzing situations. Yet even so, the outcome of most activities that take place under this Jupiteranean power are benefic and positive. *Color on the Tree*: blue. *Color Scale*: In Atziluth, a deep violet. In Briah, blue. In Yetzirah, a deep purple. In Assiah, a deep azure flecked with yellow. *Elemental Attribution*: Water. *Polarity*: as Chokmah is positive in Briah, on the subtle planes, Chesed—also on the Pillar of Mercy—is positive, masculine, and dynamic on the less subtle or less rarefied planes below the Kether-Chokmah-Binah Supernal Triad. Yet, due to the equilibrium it brings to the Tree, it possesses feminine characteristics on the less subtle and material planes of existence, as exemplified by the Water correspondence of its Elemental Attribution. *Tarot Correspondence*: The Four Fours from the Lesser Arcana.

Commentary: Again, notice how the dynamic, positive, masculine nature of Chesed is attributed to this Sephirah, despite the negative, passive, feminine characteristic of the element Water assigned to it. By doing so, the Kabbalists worked out the dual aspects of Divine manifestation below Kether: both polarities are needed for existence and expression throughout Creation, through the attainment and maintenance of equilibrium.

Geburah

Number on the Tree: Five (5). *Primary Title*: Severity. *Other Titles*: Strength; Power; Force. According to the *Sepher Yetzirah*, Geburah is called "The Radical Intelligence." *Astrological Attribution*: the planet Mars. *Intelligible Quality*: Divine Power beyond mortal comprehension. *Peak Human Experience*: the Summit of Power, perceived as a universal experience. *Sensible Qualities*: determination; perseverance; vigor; aggression; construction or destruction according to purpose; vitality; endurance. This martial planetary influence is excellent for dealing with material pursuits and matters requiring physical—as opposed to mental—energy; it is also a fortuitous time for dealing with sensual affairs of every type, problems of a mechanical nature, or working out the intellectual details of new ideas that will lead to new, mechanical inventions. Athletes, bodybuilders, and weightlifters will find this an excellent period in which to develop and shape their physical form, while effectively and safely exerting the maximum amount of energy in that physical development. The influence also provides for experimental scientific activities as opposed to purely theoretical investigations. It exerts a very adverse effect in asking for favors, or for dealing with any beneficent matters of a personal nature whatsoever. It is also a very adverse influence under which to seek or make new acquaintances with the intention of seeking favors from them at the time, or at some point in the future. It is also a very unfortunate time in which to deal with any and all legal matters, including those involving judges, courts, or attorneys in any way, as well as for gambling, speculation of any type, entering into marriage, or having surgery—whether outpatient or that requiring even the briefest period of hospitalization. The emotions are extremely volatile under this influence, particularly those of an aggressive, hostile, or violent nature. It is a time best spent alone, dealing exclusively with matters that the influence favors. *Color on the Tree*: red. *Color Scale*: In Atziluth, orange. In Briah, red. In Yetzirah, a bright, scarlet red. In Assiah, red, flecked with black. *Elemental Attribution*: Fire. *Polarity*: Negative; feminine, passive. *Tarot Correspondence*: the Four Fives of the Lesser Arcana of the deck.

Commentary: Once more, notice that Geburah (Figure 3) is on the left hand column of the Tree, and has a feminine nature, as do all of the Sephiroth in that column which is headed by Binah. Yet her attributes are decidedly male, masculine, dynamic, positive, and active, for the reason previously discussed. As such, the equilibrium of the Tree is maintained. This dynamic, masculine nature is expressed through the elemental attribution of this Sephirah, namely, Fire.

Tiphareth

Number on the Tree: Six (6). *Primary Title*: Beauty. *Other Titles*: the Mediating Intelligence; the Microprosopus or the Lesser Countenance; the Son; the Man; the Son of Man, referring to the Christ-Consciousness. *Astrological Attribution*: the Sun. *Intelligible*

Quality: Perfect Beauty; Perfect Harmony; the Ideal; the sum total of all that is Good. *Peak Human Experience of the Sephirah*: the Vision of the Harmony of all things, and through this Vision, the apprehension of or direct experience of the essence of Beauty itself. *Sensible Qualities*: the imaginative faculty of the individual; the realm of the HGA, the Holy Guardian Angel in magical literature; the point of arrival of the Abramelin Operation: an intensive, six-month magical working for attaining the K&C—Knowledge and Conversation of the Holy Guardian Angel. In the more mundane sense, owing to its Astrological Attribution, the Sun, the attributions include: power and success in life; Life itself; illumination; mental power and ability; as with Jupiter under Chesed, also money; robust physical, emotional, and mental health; growth at the personality, character, and psychic levels; dealing with superiors of all kinds, and in any situation; asking for favors from people in authority; seeking the approval, recommendation, or help from others in any proposal whatsoever, be it of a business or personal nature; composing important letters that produce in the mind of the intended recipient a picture of the writer as a confident, balanced individual whose request for aid, introductions, or favors should be immediately granted. This is also an excellent influence under which one can act in noble and high-minded ways that will build up his or her public esteem and prestige. This influence however is adverse for involving oneself in illegal plans, actions, or activities of any kind whatsoever. Curiously, it also provides a negative influence for beginning or launching a new business, a new plan, or a new idea, owing to its underlying Elemental Attribution which is always shifting, changing in force and form, as the Sun itself, the most Sensible of this Sephirothal influence that has further descended into the realm of matter. By the same rationale, it is likewise adverse for signing contracts of any kind, and for entering into any partnerships, mutually beneficial arrangements or agreement—whether of a social, business, professional, or personal nature—or for entering into any kind of relationship in which there is a political element of any kind. Additionally, this planetary influence is also quite adverse for marriage, for making any new investments of any kind, for purchasing or liquidating real estate holdings, and for all forms of surgery. *Color on the Tree*: bright yellow. *Color Scale*: In the world of Atziluth, a clear, rose pink. In Briah, a golden yellow. In Yetzirah, a rich, salmon pink. In Assiah, a golden amber. *Elemental Attribution*: Air. *Polarity*: None, as Tiphareth is the product of the positive, masculine polarity of Chesed, and the negative, feminine polarity of Geburah, acting in equilibrium and unison to project this central point of the Tree. *Tarot Correspondence*: the Four Sixes of the Lesser Arcana of the deck.

Netzach

Number on the Tree: Seven (7). *Primary Title*: Victory. *Other Titles*: the *Sepher Yetzirah* gives this Sephirah the title of "The Occult Intelligence." Also, Eternity; Triumph; Firmness. *Astrological Attribution*: the planet Venus. *Intelligible Quality*: the Vision of Beauty Triumphant. *Peak Human Experience of this Sephirah*: the Experience of Beauty Triumphant. *Sensible Qualities*: Unselfishness; Love, but of a sexual nature; beauty of form, and the appreciation of that beauty; the emotions of the conscious level of our being; women; music; self-indulgence; extravagance. Also on the mundane level, this influence governs all material and sensual affairs; music; art; the theater; any form of behavior or expression that supports sensuality. It is also a very fortuitous influence under which to begin any new enterprise or project, whether sensual or business in nature. It is also an excellent influence in which to make new acquaintances, but only those that are met through spontaneous social contact. It is also a very favorable influence for entering into marriage, to borrow or loan money, and to host social gatherings and parties, but only those affairs that are meant for pure enjoyment. It is very positive for speculating in stocks, bonds, or in any new business proposition. It is important to note here that due to the Venusian planetary influence of this Sephirah, almost any activity or action that is begun or ended while this influence is in operation, will bear very significant, desirable, or fortunate results. It is an influence that, in effect, blesses and magnifies activities of almost any kind, but especially those of a sensual and material nature. There are a few very adverse aspects of this influence, such as dealing with social underlings or subordinates; beginning long trips to remote locations; using social means to harm enemies or competitors, or to attempt using social functions as a means of gaining a business or personal advantage at the expense of a collaborator or fellow worker. *Color on the Tree*:

green. *Color Scale*: In Atziluth, amber. In Briah, emerald. In Yetzirah, bright yellow-green. In Assiah, olive, flecked with gold. *Elemental Attribution*: Fire. *Polarity*: Masculine, positive. *Tarot Correspondence*: the Four Sevens of the Lesser Arcana of the deck.

Hod

Number on the Tree: Eight (8). *Primary Title*: Splendor. *Other Titles*: Glory; the *Yetziratic* Text calls Hod the "Absolute or Perfect Intelligence." *Astrological Attribution*: the planet Mercury. *Intelligible Quality*: the Vision of Splendor. *Peak Human Experience*: once again, according to the Yetziratic Text, Hod is called the Perfect Intelligence, because it is power in a state of equilibrium. For the individual to experience this state is to attain the peak experience of this Sephirah. *Sensible Qualities*: On the higher levels, Truthfulness and Honesty are two of the blessings of this Sephirah, along with the philosophic and laboratory pursuit of Alchemy. On the more mundane levels, this Mercurial influence is very positive for dealing with intellectual discernments; scientific thought; mathematics; writing of all kinds; logic; reason; using and accelerating the analytical faculty of the conscious self; thinking; speaking, whether in public or private. Additionally, as with Netzach and Venus, the Mercurial influence of Hod is very beneficial for art, music, and the theater; for literary work of any kind; to design or begin new advertising efforts; to plan new projects or involvements; to launch new business plans; to make new acquaintances in business or academic circles, and to begin new business relationships. It is an excellent influence under which one can successfully initiate contracts, but short-term ones only. It is also an excellent time for reading or buying new books that can be of great help to the individual in an intellectual, life-sustaining, or life-enhancing way; also for dealing with business or academic journals, papers, or researching documents, such as land and property Title and Deed searches. This influence also favors educational matters of every type, as well as the buying and selling of printed material. It imparts a very benefic influence for taking any medicine or beginning any system of mental cure. It is an excellent influence for mystical, metaphysical, or magical study, under which profound insight into occult, esoteric, mystical, or magical concepts can be achieved, the essence of which can be then used for intellectual growth, the attainment of considerable material benefit, or both. It is also a positive influence for speculating and taking chances in a business or proposition that at other times may appear unsound or chancy. This is also an excellent influence under which important letters can be written. This Mercurial influence has some serious negative aspects as well, such as dealing with enemies in any legal manner; entering into marriage, or in seeking favors from people in authority. It is equally adverse for either purchasing or selling real estate holdings, and is a period in which the individual can become the target of fraudulent or even illegal schemes. In general, it is an influence under which the truthfulness of all statements coming from anyone must be carefully evaluated, despite the overall positive aspects this influence exerts. *Color on the Tree*: orange. *Color Scale*: In Atziluth, a violet-purple. In Briah, orange. In Yetzirah, a russet-red. In Assiah, a yellowish-black or brown flecked with white. *Elemental Attribution*: Water (feminine, creative, passive, negative). *Polarity*: Negative (feminine). *Tarot Correspondence*: the Four Eights of the Lesser Arcana of the deck.

Yesod

Number on the Tree: Nine (9). *Primary Title*: the Foundation. *Other Titles*: the Anima Mundi, or the Soul of the World; also the "Pure Intelligence or Clear Intelligence." *Astrological Attribution*: the Moon (Luna). *Intelligible Quality*: the Divine Cognition of the working of the universe. *Peak Human Experience of this Sephirah*: the Vision or Experience of the working of the universe. *Sensible Qualities*: according to the *Yetziratic* Text, Yesod purifies the emanations received from the other Sephiroth, as it is the receptacle of all of the emanations from the other eight spheres above it. Additionally, since Yesod is the sole focus of the other Sephiroth emanations, it is the sole projector of those forces into the world of matter: the physical plane of Malkuth. It is also the Astral Plane of occultism, and the realm of the Astral Light. It is the sphere of Magic as well, as all operations of a magical nature that are intended to produce an effect in Malkuth, have their foundations in this Sephirah. On the daily, more pragmatic level, the planetary attribution of Yesod, the Moon, takes the correspondences of, and produces its influence upon: women; the personality; modifications; rapid changes; fluid conditions, ever cycling between extremes. As with Hod's projection, Mercury, educational efforts of all kinds are also ruled by the Moon, it being the projection of Yesod into our universe. Additionally, this lunar influence provides a positive impulse for the planting of seeds, beginning journeys by water, or making new acquaintances in a social, business, or academic setting. It is also an excellent influence for all literary work, for entering into the sacrament of marriage, for taking any medicine, or to begin any mystical or metaphysical system of body or mind treatment in which a direct, complete cure is sought. This Lunar influence of Yesod is also very positive for surgery of all types, and for dealing with metaphysical, mystical, and magical studies. This fluid, creative, Lunar influence provides an energy dynamic backdrop against which most activities and aspirations indulged in during the time of its reign will prove both prolific and productive. *Color on the Tree*: purple. *Color Scale*: In Atziluth, indigo. In Briah, violet. In Yetzirah, a very dark purple. In Assiah, a citrine flecked with azure. *Elemental Attribution*: as with Tiphareth, the elemental attribution of Yesod is Air, owing to its position on the Middle Pillar of the Tree. *Polarity*: Neutral. *Tarot Correspondence*: the Four Nines of the Lesser Arcana of the deck.

Commentary: *Notice, that as with Yesod and the other Sephirah on the Middle Pillar, Kether also takes the elemental attribution of Air as well. This is thought to be due to the impulsive, ever-changing, fluid, potential–to–kinetic and back again dynamics of this Air element, but in its most pure, rarefied, and complete form in the case of Kether. In Yesod however, these transitional properties of the Air Element can be seen as being reflected directly into Malkuth, where they become more stable by virtue of their appearance in the densest, most material form of matter— the physical matter which is found in Malkuth.*

Malkuth

Number on the Tree: Ten (10). *Primary Title*: the Kingdom. *Other Titles*: the World of the Four Elements—Air, Earth, Water, and Fire; the "Resplendent Intelligence," because as Fortune has reflected, it is exalted above every head and sits upon the Throne of Binah. Also, The Gate of Justice; the Gate of the Daughter of the Mighty One; the Gate of Prayer; the Gate of the Shadow of Death and of Death itself; the Gate of the Garden of Eden; the Queen; the

Bride; the Inferior Mother. *Astrological Attribution*: the Element, Earth, but divided into four quadrants, representing the World of the Four Elements: Air, Earth, Water, and Fire. That is, matter in its entirety, yet not simply the gross form that composes matter as we perceive it with our five senses. The other subtle psychic qualities of the Four Elements are also included in this attribution, namely, the subtle, psychic aspects of Air, Earth, Water, and Fire. These too are encompassed by Malkuth. *Intelligible Quality*: the Existence and Projection of the Psychic and Mundane Essences of Four Elements into the realm of Malkuth. *Peak Human Experience of this Sephirah*: the Vision of the Holy Guardian Angel. *Sensible Qualities*: discernment; astuteness; acute sensory perception of ordinary matter. The physical performance of the Abramelin Operation, leading to the Vision of the HGA, and the Attainment of the Knowledge and Conversation of the HGA while the individual is yet in human form (see Commentary below). *Color on the Tree*: the tenth Sephirah is divided by an 'X' into four equal sections in order to bisect the sphere. The colors olive, russet, citrine, and black are then assigned, one color to each of the four equal sections. *Color Scale*: In the Atziluthic World, a clear yellow. In Briatic World, olive, russet, citrine, and black. In the Yetziratic World, olive, russet, citrine, and black, flecked with gold. In the Assiatic World, black, rayed with yellow. *Elemental Attribution*: Earth (as described above). *Polarity*: Neutral. The grounding-point of the purified emanations from all of the other Sephiroth, radiating from Yesod into Malkuth. *Tarot Attribution*: the Four Tens of the Lesser Arcana of the deck.

Commentary: There is a difficult point here regarding the mystical relationship between Tiphareth and Malkuth of the Middle Pillar, which some readers may need to understand clearly for their Kabbalistic studies and beyond. Specifically, it involves the concept of the 'True Will,' the Holy Guardian Angel (HGA), and the Attainment of the Knowledge and Conversation (K&C) of the HGA through the magical working of the Abramelin Operation.

The True Will of the individual; that is, the Will of God for the individual, is identified with the Chiah. In turn, the Chiah is the essential energy of that part of the self which is eternal. But the realm of the HGA who delivers the True Will to the individual, is that of Tiphareth. Here, the HGA is considered by some to be the Higher Self: a type of pure consciousness so exalted as to be above the everyday reach of the individual.

Fortune said of it, "…it is an intensification of awareness…" and from it "…comes a peculiar power of insight and penetration which is of the nature of hyper-developed intuition." [24]

Thus, in some occult circles and magical societies, it is conceived of as the elevation of the individual's highest qualities, raised to the nth level, yet partaking of divine qualities by its very definition. While the Experience of the HGA most certainly does exhibit this divine state that does lie beyond ecstasy—which quickly transforms into an Experience of Divine Love and Beauty beyond description—it is my opinion that Fortune's viewpoint is far, far, from the sum total of the experience of Attaining to the Knowledge and Conversation of the HGA.

In point of fact, the HGA is an individual being with its own universe, holding an utterly profound and nebulous personal consciousness of its own, yet with a conscious awareness of the individual human being over which it presides. Hence, it is through the Abramelin Operation, conducted physically in Malkuth according to the Abramelin text, that the individual does attain to the actual, physical Vision of the HGA, which is then immediately followed by the Attainment to the **full** K&C of this being.

In other words, both Fortune's view of the HGA's nature and the individual's experience of it as I have laid down herein, are valid in my opinion. That is, through the classical performance of the Abramelin Operation, the individual calls down the True Will from Chokmah into Malkuth, as that True Will has manifested in the centralized focus of Tiphareth, and through the being of the HGA. Through this act, the Godhead of Chokmah—as projected from Kether—is brought down into Manhood—into Malkuth—through the intervention of the Holy Guardian Angel in Tiphareth.

At the same time, Manhood, existing in Malkuth, is elevated into Godhead, through the agency of the HGA, in Tiphareth. And so the ancient admonition, "Bring Godhead down into manhood, and elevate manhood into Godhead," is fulfilled. It is a fundamental error to think however, as Dion Fortune herself so unfortunately states later on in her classic book on Kabbalah, that the HGA "…consists neither in voices nor visions, but is pure consciousness…" [24]

Why is this error so dangerous? Because the state of the individual's subjective synthesis is effected thereby, precluding the actual Vision of the HGA. This occurs through the very acceptance of her point of view: an attitude engendered, projected, and maintained by mainstream New Age Magick. As a result of accepting this limiting viewpoint, the individual can only attain to a partial experience of the HGA; a partial result that ends more often than not in hallucinations regarding the experience, and confusion as to the individual's *full* True Will.

In more applicable terms, this error in understanding can cause difficulties in the diligent individual's formation of his or her subjective state; one that can produce subconscious errors in the use of the Kabbalah proper.

There is no need for an either-or scenario as so many magical schools, occult circles, want-to-be, self-professed magicians, and occultists insist, all as a result of never having attempted the Abramelin Operation, let alone having Attained to the *full* K&C of the HGA. But then, it is only through the direct Experience of Attaining to the *full* K&C of the HGA, and this by attaining to the Vision of this being in Malkuth, that this simple understanding can become known.

Chapter Five

Concerning the Paths of the Holy Tree of Life

In order to fully comprehend the Kabbalah, most of the components of that system must be made known to some extent on a first exposure. This is not simply to build and strengthen the individual's state of subjective synthesis (as important as that is), but to provide him or her with the necessary tools to apply this system correctly in daily life: be it in the individual's mundane affairs, or in magical matters. For I wanted to wait until now to mention something. The Kabbalah is not limited exclusively to magical work alone, as my second book, *Kabbalistic Cycles and the Mastery of Life* has shown. If you use the Kabbalah correctly, you will find that it will work perfectly for you in every area of your life. Have I made a typing mistake—or worse yet—an error of the ego by making such a claim? Something that will work one hundred percent of the time?

There is no error here. It is as simple as this. Learn the Kabbalah as presented in this book, for the time being, before moving on to a further study of it. Learn the Sensible Qualities of each Sephirah and those of the Paths that follow this discussion, apply that knowledge by *discovering the techniques of its application to both your magical and extra-magical activities on your own*, or through consulting the book just mentioned, and you will find my statement to be one hundred percent accurate. Period. People will argue the point that nothing is ever one hundred percent! My response to that is twofold.

First, it's not that things are not one hundred percent. If you look even casually at any situation, you will find it is *people* that are not one hundred percent. Why? Because most individuals truly expect something for nothing. Or more usually, they expect something to work one hundred percent of the time after learning it in a slipshod fashion, and then applying it in a casual, shoddy way. Then of course they complain, "Well, I tried it, and as usual with these things, it doesn't work the way I wanted it to!" The key word in that statement is 'as usual,' because their learning, effort in application, and habit patterns are slipshod and shabby, 'as usual.'

Secondly, it has always been my position that anything in the occult or magical worlds should and must work with regularity and precision, as surely as do the Laws of Nature I study and experiment with as a physicist. If they do not—if it seems that there are too many variables as the New Agers so love to proffer as an excuse—or equally, that the occult and magic are Arts and not a Science as that tepid group also loves to use as a rationale for their lack of results, then it would be madness for anyone to devote a significant portion of their life to the study and practice of such flippant, *causally unconnected* 'disciplines.'

The truth of it is that the occult in general, and magic in particular, are the same as any of the hard sciences. They have as much of an artful twist, as they do a rigorous, logical, repeatable, scientific base. This understanding on the part of the reader will enable him or her to exercise their natural flare and variations in using any occult or magical technique—that artful twist—while yet assuring the outcome of that technique through the scientifically applied logical, rigorous, repeatable base.

There you have it. Use your artful flare, but only through your scientific application: an application/technique that can only come by understanding and rigorously applying the underlying principles of whatever occult or magical work you are involved in— and your Kabbalistic Analysis will give you this, as you should know by now. If you do, I further guarantee that you will find there truly are *principles* underlying *any and all* occult and magical work. If you heed this counsel, I promise that you will succeed in your magical rituals and extra-magical affairs, one hundred percent of the time. So please pay close attention, and let's proceed.

Now, as both the Intellectual and Sensible qualities and correspondences of each Sephirah were given, we will now concern ourselves with the Intelligible and Sensible qualities and attributes of the Paths. Remember too, that since the Kabbalah can be used in your daily life as well as in your practical magical working, the

Sensible characteristics of the Paths—as with the Sephiroth—will eventually become your prime focus as far as your daily life matters are concerned.

For now, however, it is important that you understand, or at least are made aware of, both their Intelligible and Sensible attributions. And as promised, after you have also been exposed to the mystical—that is, the Intelligible—basis of the Paths, we will add *the fundamental correspondence* traditionally assigned to them in the next chapter: their Tarot Attributions. For these will enable you to perform Path Working Magic in an entirely new way. A way that is extremely effective, and which produces immediate psychic results that will—in turn—enormously enhance your overall magical work.

The Tarot can also be used as a 'back door' method by which the practitioner can gain access to the Sephiroth; this, through the corresponding Path attributed to a specific Tarot card, should he or she wish to experiment in this form of magic. Both of these considerations will be discussed in the opening remarks of Chapter Six. In effect then, after completing this book, your newly acquired knowledge of the Tree of Life will then be used as a template that will enable you to build up your Kabbalistic Knowledge System, step-by-step.

In point of fact, you have probably realized that you have been building up this system while studying this book so far, and indeed you have. After Chapter Six gives you the *fundamental correspondence* to the Paths and discusses their importance, Chapter Seven will round out your practical understanding of the Kabbalah, enabling you to work with various materials that are desirable in ritual practices, and which are absolutely necessary in ceremonial rites. With these promises now made to you, let us now proceed to our investigation of the Paths of the Tree of Life.

There are a number of factors I ask the reader to keep in mind as we explore the Paths and their attributions. First of all, as with the Sephiroth, please remember that only a very limited number of attributions and qualities of the Paths are given here. The reader's study of the previously recommended texts will greatly increase this list of attributions. As that list grows, so will your comprehension of the concepts. In turn, as your comprehension increases, so will your understanding and apprehension.

Secondly, and again as with the Sephiroth attributions and correspondences, kindly remember that I did not formulate or derive the attributions of the Paths that will follow. They are general characteristics of these interconnections between the Sephiroth that are distributed or cited in one form or another throughout the voluminous tomes of occult, magical, mystical, and metaphysical literature.

Third, be warned if you are new to Kabbalah, you may find that the Paths have a plethora of attributions and characteristics which may sound redundant or repetitive. For example, with Path Number Eleven, you will find its astrological correspondence to be that of the Element Air, while for Path 12, you will find its astrological attribution to be Mercury, which has already been assigned to the Sephirah Hod. And of course, there is a correlation between Air, Mercury, and Hod. So what does this mean? (As part of your Kabbalistic training, I invite the student to think about this seeming innocuous correlation.) This is not some Kabbalistic slight-of-hand, but rather, an assigned characteristic based upon specific aspects of the natures of the Sephiroth connected by these Paths.

Additionally, these seeming repeated correspondences have higher meanings when applied to the Paths, owing to the exalted natures of the Sephiroth connected by them. In other words, these higher octaves of the correspondences are actually referring to the *Intelligible Quality* of each Sephirah being connected by a specific Path. But all of this will be discovered by you as you wade through all the books recommended for further study.

Please also be aware that even though the Intelligible Quality must be firmly rooted in your mind, we will be paying special attention to the *fundamental correspondence: the Tarot.* After all, we eventually need to become *practical,* and we will do so because this *fundamental correspondence* applies to the *Sensible Qualities* of the *Paths only,* which are *the* attributions you will be using in much of your practical magical work, *and* in the application of the Kabbalah to your daily life. It would be a wise move on the part of the reader to pause at this point, and reread and contemplate what has just been stated. It will pay big dividends as you proceed through the Paths.

Previously, I mentioned that there are twenty-two paths on the Tree, and that the connecting Paths indicate and explain the relationship that any two given Sephiroth bear to each other. But in fact, there are *thirty-two* paths. How can this be? *Because each Sephirah is considered to be a Path as well.* Why is this so? To be sure, there are several explanations for this, all of which are interesting and theoretically sound, as a review of any of the recommended texts will reveal.

In terms of a *daily working model* however, I prefer my own concept. *I prefer to think of each Sephirah as a Path, due to its **Sensible qualities,** which are those more mundane or earthy correspondences, attributes, and governances that are ascribed to each Sephirah.* Put another way, if the reader will accept this working model and definition, then it is not difficult to understand that the Path influence of each Sephirah is simply due to the modus operandi which enables a Sephirah to have an effect in the World of Malkuth.

In this case, it is the planetary or other *projections* of each Sephirah, referred to as the Astrological Attribution in the section on the Sephiroth. If the reader reviews the *Sensible Qualities* of the Sephiroth given earlier, he or she will see that in the case of Binah through Yesod, the planetary projections of these Sephiroth are classically and historically assigned as the influences that project the lower qualities of these Sephiroth into the everyday world in which we live, move, and have our being—the World of Malkuth.

Thus, for Binah, Saturn is the planetary force that projects the attributions of the more mundane aspects of this planet into our world. For Chesed, Jupiter is assigned, and so on, until we finally end in Malkuth (Earth). In the cases of Kether and Chokmah, where there are no planetary attributions given, it nevertheless becomes easy for us to understand the Sensible Qualities given, owing to the extrapolations made from the nature of these higher Sephiroth. In the case of Malkuth, our understanding that it is the focal point of all the previous Sephirothal projections, including the planetary projections that came before it, that provides us insight into its Sensible state.

If this is the case and all of the Seven Planets of the Ancients— as the planetary projections Saturn, Jupiter, Mars, the Sun, Venus, Mercury and the Moon are termed in occult literature—have already been assigned to Binah through Yesod, then where are the projectors of the remaining twenty-two Paths that provide their projections into the lower or more mundane World of Malkuth, as did the Sephiroth? To answer this question, a few other salient facts must be addressed.

First off, we must consider the attributable characteristics or correspondences spoken of above which are assigned to the Paths by the Classical Kabbalah. The manner of such assignment is accomplished by designating one of the twenty-two letters of the Hebrew alphabet to each Path. This can be a type of convention for naming a Path, if you will, and for building a foundation upon which one can gain an understanding of the multiple meanings and ideas of a given Path, along with the spiritual or psychic forces that Path is said to represent.

These letters have five basic characteristics, or additional attributions assigned to them. I am also assigning the classical Kabbalistic quality of a Basal Attribute as another correspondence of each Path: be this attribution planetary, elemental, or zodiacal. This Basal Attribute corresponds to the Sensible qualities of the Path, while the Occult Concept corresponds to the Intelligible qualities, and lends a feeling for the Mystical and Symbolic Meaning of the Path. Lastly, by stating the obvious, I refer to each Path by a Path Name, derived by simply naming each Path according to the name of the Hebrew letter assigned to it.

Taken together, these eight characteristics will embody a view of the individual and collective concepts of a Path, in addition to establishing a procedure for us to add to those meanings based upon our own individual mystical, magical, metaphysical, and daily life experiences.

The five 'standard' characteristics of each of the twenty-two Hebrew letters are:

- Path Number on the Tree.
- A specific position in the alphabet. For example, first letter of the alphabet, fourth letter of the alphabet, and so on.
- A numerical value of the letter.
- A symbolical meaning applied to the Path.
- A Tarot card attribution of the Path.

A discussion of each of these five characteristics relative to each Path, along with the Path Name, Basal Attribute and Occult Concept, now follows. As the reader will come to understand by the end of this section, however, there is *one and only one* of these eight correspondences that will be used in practical magical performance as—for example—in Path Working Magic. Nevertheless, for the sake of subjective synthesis, all will be presented and briefly reviewed.

Since there are thirty-two Paths on the Tree, and since each Sephirah is also considered to be a Path in its own right, the convention of listing the Paths begins with Path Number Eleven (11) and follows sequentially down the Tree. In addition, by assigning a Hebrew letter to each Path, it becomes easy for us to learn the Paths by simply calling or referring to each Path by its Hebrew letter. Using this mental code, you will be amazed at how quickly this schema will enable you to master the Occult Meaning behind the Tree, along with its multitude of correspondences.

Lastly, remember that the Tarot Attribution of each Path applies to the twenty-two cards of the Greater Arcana or the Trumps Major, and not the cards of the Four Suits (the Lesser Arcana). In terms of the five characteristics of the twenty-two Hebrew letters, the Path Names, Basal Attributions and the Occult Concepts, we can now begin the study of the Paths. (Please refer to Figure 3 in Chapter Four).

• *Path Number on the Tree*: Eleven (**11**), connecting Kether and Chokmah.

Path Name: Aleph (Hebrew letter, 'A'), meaning, the head of an Ox. *Position of Hebrew letter in alphabet*: First, or One (1). *Numerical Value of Hebrew letter*: 1 (One). *Symbolic Meaning of Path*: "The Scintillating Intelligence." *Occult Concept of Path*: the primeval movement of the Great, Creative Breath, spinning the chaos from the moment of Creation into a creative core. *Basal Attribute of the Path*: the Element, Air. *Tarot Attribution of Path*: Tarot Trump, Zero (O) — The Fool.

• *Path Number on the Tree*: Twelve (**12**), connecting Kether and Binah.

Path Name: Beth (Hebrew letter, 'B'), meaning, House. *Position of Hebrew letter in alphabet*: Second, or Two (2). *Numerical Value of Hebrew letter*: 2 (Two). *Symbolic Meaning of Path*: "The Transparent Intelligence." *Occult Concept of Path*: the combined natures of the Sephiroth Chokmah and Hod are reflected by this Path. Their properties are Mercurial; here, in an alchemical sense of Universal Mercury, as hinted at in the section on Hod. That is, due to the higher octave of this Path, the Mercurial nature expressed here is more in line with the Intelligible Quality found in the Mercury of the Philosophers, which can be reached through the higher aspects of the Sensible Qualities of Hod: Initiated working in the realms of Philosophic *and* Laboratory Alchemy. This Mercurial Principle is therefore that living, ever-changing Principle of cohesive force that holds all of Creation together, from the subtlest of matter to its most material of form. *Basal Attribute of Path*: the planet, Mercury, but with the understanding given above. *Tarot Attribution of Path*: Tarot Trump, One (I) — The Magician.

• **Path Number on the Tree**: Thirteen (**13**), connecting Kether and Tiphareth.

Path Name: Gimel (Hebrew letter, 'G'), meaning Camel. *Position of Hebrew letter in alphabet*: Third, or Three (3). *Numerical Value of Hebrew letter*: 3 (Three). *Symbolic Meaning of Path*: "The Uniting Intelligence." *Occult Concept of Path*: The portal of entry into an Inner Magical Sanctum or College of the Masters, as understood by advanced practitioners of Magic. *Basal Attribute of the Path*: the 'planet' Moon. *Tarot Attribution of Path*: Tarot Trump, Two (II) — The High Priestess.

• **Path Number on the Tree**: Fourteen (**14**), connecting Chokmah and Binah.

Path Name: Daleth (Hebrew letter 'D'), meaning, Door. *Position of Hebrew letter in alphabet*: Fourth, or Four (4). *Numerical Value of Hebrew letter*: 4 (Four). *Symbolic Meaning of Path*: "The Luminous Intelligence." *Occult Concept of Path*: The force by which opposites are attracted to each other. Due to the Basal Attribute assigned to this Path, the implication is one of Love, although in a higher aspect. In this instance, a Love whose end result of uniting the opposites, produces a mystical creation and experience through the act of union. *Basal Attribute of the Path*: the planet, Venus. *Tarot Attribution of Path*: Tarot Trump, Three (III) — The Empress.

• **Path Number on the Tree**: Fifteen (**15**), connecting Chokmah and Tiphareth.

Path Name: Heh (Hebrew letter 'H'), meaning, Window. *Position of Hebrew letter in alphabet*: Fifth, or Five (5). *Numerical Value of Hebrew letter*: 5 (Five). *Symbolic Meaning of Path*: "The Constituting Intelligence." *Occult Concept of Path*: Although many martial characteristics are applied to this Path due to its Basal Attribution, the higher aspect of this Path is of more interest and use to us here. This Path is associated with the alchemical Principle of the Sulphur, itself a fire related concept exhibiting energy, and the penetrative dynamics of the mind, the mental dynamics being equally fiery when used properly. Why this latter correspondence? Because to those initiated into Alchemy, the alchemical Sulphur possesses a physical vehicle, the exact nature of which depends upon which of the Three Kingdoms of Nature from which it is extracted. It is this vehicle which embodies and actually contains the *consciousness* of the substance being worked upon alchemically. *Basal Attribute of the Path*: the Zodiacal Sign of Aries. *Tarot Attribution of Path*: Tarot Trump, Four (IV) — The Emperor.

• *Path Number on the Tree*: Sixteen (**16**), connecting Chokmah and Chesed.

Path Name: Vav (Hebrew letter 'V'), meaning, a Nail. *Position of Hebrew letter in alphabet*: Sixth, or Six (6). *Numerical Value of Hebrew letter*: 6 (Six). *Symbolic Meaning of Path*: "The Son of Tetragrammaton." *Occult Concept of Path*: In its higher aspects, this Path is symbolic of the act of Redemption, and the Joy that issues from that redemption. *Basal Attribute of the Path*: the Zodiacal Sign of Taurus. *Tarot Attribution of Path*: Tarot Trump, Five (V) — The Hierophant.

• *Path Number on the Tree*: Seventeen (**17**), connecting Binah and Tiphareth.

Path Name: Zayin (Hebrew letter 'Z'), meaning, Sword. *Position of Hebrew letter in alphabet*: Seventh, or Seven (7). *Numerical Value of Hebrew letter*: 7 (Seven). *Symbolic Meaning of Path*: "The Disposing Intelligence." *Occult Concept of Path*: Again, in its higher aspects, this Path is symbolic of the Primal Force behind all of the fabricating and forging forces within Nature, and is symbolic of the depths of the consciousness of Nature itself. *Basal Attribute of the Path*: The Zodiacal Sign of Gemini. *Tarot Attribution of Path*: Tarot Trump Six (VI)—The Lovers.

• *Path Number on the Tree*: Eighteen (**18**), connecting Binah and Geburah.

Path Name: Cheth, pronounced using the guttural 'Ck' sound made in pronouncing the word 'rock' (Hebrew letter 'CH'), meaning, Fence. *Position of Hebrew letter in alphabet*: Eighth, or Eight (8). *Numerical Value of Hebrew letter*: 8 (Eight). *Symbolic Meaning of Path*: "The House of Influence." The process by which accomplishing the Great Work itself. Also the Work, Devotion, Dedication, Comprehension and Understanding, by which one comes to grasp the reality of Kether, through the Accomplishment of the Great Work. *Occult Concept of Path*: the first step of the process in the Attainment of the Great Work, which is the Attainment of the Knowledge and Conversation (K&C) of the Holy Guardian Angel (HGA). *Basal Attribute of the Path*: the Zodiacal Sign of Cancer. *Tarot Attribution of Path*: Tarot Trump Seven (VII) — The Chariot.

• *Path Number on the Tree*: Nineteen (**19**), connecting Chesed and Geburah.

Path Name: Teth (Hebrew letter 'T'), meaning, Serpent. *Position of Hebrew letter in alphabet*: Ninth, or Nine (9). *Numerical Value of Hebrew letter*: 9 (Nine). *Symbolic Meaning of Path*: I refer to this Path as "The Alternate Path," uniting the opposites of the male potency of Chesed, with the female potency of Geburah; the Path joining the opposites of Mercy and Severity, as shown by the Chesedian-placement on the Pillar of Mercy, and the Geburahian-situated Sephirah on the Pillar of Severity. *Occult Concept of Path*: Although the Serpent is assigned to this Path due to its association with Teth, the Lion is also a corollary of this connecting pathway between Chesed and Geburah. In the higher aspects of this Path's meaning, it is the Lion which is of interest here, having a very special meaning in Alchemy: the production of—at first a menstrum—termed the "Green Lion," from which the Stone of the Wise is eventually produced. By allegory, it also has implication for that psycho-spiritual process of self-transformation through which the 'lead' of Man's lower nature is transmuted and united with the Higher Nature that dwells within the deepest recesses of the Self. *Basal Attribute of the Path*: the Zodiacal Sign of Leo. *Tarot Attribution of Path*: Tarot Trump, Eight (VIII) — Strength.

• *Path Number on the Tree*: Twenty (**20**), connecting Chesed and Tiphareth.

Path Name: Yod (Hebrew letters 'I', 'Y'), meaning, a Hand, but with the index finger pointing, and the other fingers closed, forming a Fist, which is also the meaning of this Path. *Position of Hebrew letter in alphabet*: Tenth, or Ten (10). *Numerical Value of Hebrew letter*: 10 (Ten). *Symbolic Meaning of Path*: "The Forceful Intelligence," as I term this Path, owing to the nature of its higher meaning, as given in the Occult Concept. *Occult Concept of Path*: The movement of the One Consciousness through which the forces of the universe have been set in motion. *Basal Attribute of the Path*: the Zodiacal Sign of Virgo. *Tarot Attribution of Path*: Tarot Trump, Nine (IX) — The Hermit.

• *Path Number on the Tree*: Twenty-One (**21**), connecting Chesed and Netzach.

Path Name: Kaph (Hebrew letter 'K'), meaning, a cupped hand, or spoon. *Position of Hebrew letter in alphabet*: Eleventh, or Eleven (11). *Numerical Value of Hebrew letter*: 20 (Twenty). *Symbolic Meaning of Path*: "The Conciliatory Intelligence." *Occult Concept of Path*: With its higher aspects through its Intelligible Quality of the pure, expansive, open nature of Chesed to its Sensible Jupiteranean influence which is eventually united or conciliated with the Intelligible Quality of Netzach, being the Vision of Beauty, it is then expressed in the World of Malkuth through the Venusian Sensible Quality of Love. In effect, a conciliation occurs between the Sensible Qualities projected by the planetary attributions of these two Sephiroth into the lower worlds. Yet, this same act of conciliation also occurs between the higher aspects of these two Sephiroth. What we have as a result of this conciliatory act is a balance between the Intelligible and Sensible Qualities of these spheres, each on their own plane, yet complementing each other on their respective planes of existence through the nature of this Path. *Basal Attribute of the Path*: the planet, Jupiter. *Tarot Attribution of Path*: Tarot Trump, Ten (X) — The Wheel of Fortune.

• *Path Number on the Tree*: Twenty-Two (**22**), connecting Geburah and Tiphareth.

Path Name: Lamed (Hebrew letter 'L'), meaning, a Whip. *Position of Hebrew letter in alphabet*: Twelfth, or Twelve (12). *Numerical Value of Hebrew letter*: 30 (Thirty). *Symbolic Meaning of Path*: "The Faithful Intelligence." *Occult Concept of Path*: This Path has a combined meaning, much as did Kaph. Here we find the higher aspects of balance, justice, equity, and law, but ruling not only in the higher realms, but dispensing its lawful decrees in the world of Men through action/reaction. In this way, the Path exerts a leveling influence on the actions of mankind through a cause/effect relationship. The results stemming directly from those actions are thus brought about without regard to emotional appeal, social convention, or excuse. *Basal Attribute of the Path*: the Zodiacal Sign of Libra. *Tarot Attribution of Path*: Tarot Trump, Eleven (XI) — Justice.

• *Path Number on the Tree*: Twenty-Three (**23**), connecting Geburah and Hod.

Path Name: Mem (Hebrew letter 'M'), meaning, Water. *Position of Hebrew letter in alphabet*: Thirteenth of Thirteen (13). *Numerical Value of Hebrew letter*: 40 (Forty). *Symbolic Meaning of Path*: "The Stable Intelligence." *Occult Concept of Path*: The higher aspects of this Path refers to Mankind in a state of sin, unredeemed, but possessing that spiritual nature which will lead him to his ultimate Salvation. *Basal Attribute of the Path*: the Element, Water. *Tarot Attribution of Path*: Tarot Trump, Twelve (XII) — The Hanged Man.

• *Path Number on the Tree*: Twenty-Four (**24**), connecting Tiphareth and Netzach.

Path Name: Nun (Hebrew letter 'N'), meaning, Fish. *Position of Hebrew letter in alphabet*: Fourteenth, or Fourteen (14). *Numerical Value of Hebrew letter*: 50 (Fifty). *Symbolic Meaning of Path*: "The Imaginative Intelligence." *Occult Concept of Path*: The higher aspects of this Path have a two-fold attribution. The first is reflective of the alchemical process of Putrefaction that leads to the stage of Regeneration. In this case, reference is made to the Work on the Stone of the Wise. Through this process, the former *physical*, putrefied base material is exalted through a spiritual unfoldment and psychic development on the part of the alchemist, eventually leading to *the* physical manifestation of the Philosophic Substance in the laboratory. This is a highly elevated activity of the Sensible Qualities of this Path. It is this laboratory operation that combines the unfoldment of the alchemist with the 'first part' of the laboratory alchemical act—using the "First Trinity Process" as I term it—of Maceration, Digestion, and Cohobation, to produce the Black Dragon. This seemingly dead substance is then used to produce the Philosophic Substance through the "Second Trinity Process" of Separation, Purification, and Cohobation. The second meaning of this Path is its reference to the spiritual process which mirrors the laboratory process exactly: The Dark Night of the Soul, a time in which the individual undergoes the stages of Separation, Purification, and Cohobation, but within his or her own nature, so that the Light of the Spirit within them becomes manifest throughout their entire nature: physical, psychic, and spiritual. *Basal Attribute of the Path*: the Zodiacal Sign of Scorpio. *Tarot Attribution of Path*: Tarot Trump, Thirteen (XIII) — Death.

• *Path Number on the Tree*: Twenty-Five (**25**), connecting Tiphareth and Yesod.

Path Name: Samech (Hebrew letter 'S'), meaning, Prop. *Position of Hebrew letter in alphabet*: Fifteenth, or Fifteen (15). *Numerical Value of Hebrew letter*: 60 (Sixty). *Symbolic Meaning of Path*: "The Tentative Intelligence." *Occult Concept of Path*: Once again, in its higher aspect, the individual's ascent to the Holy Guardian Angel is implied by this Path. Notice the 'upward' movement from Yesod into Tiphareth: the latter being the realm of the HGA. The ascent is thereby through the world of Yesod, the foundation for all magic that is to have an effect in the world of Malkuth. (See entry under **Yesod** in the section on the Sephiroth.) Yesod also takes the correspondence of the unconscious mind, that gateway leading to the realm of ritual and ceremonial magic, and through them, upward toward the HGA. *Basal Attribute of the Path*: the Zodiacal Sign of Sagittarius. *Tarot Attribution of Path*: Tarot Trump, Fourteen (XIV) — Temperance.

• *Path Number on the Tree*: Twenty-Six (**26**), connecting Tiphareth and Hod.

Path Name: Ayin (Hebrew letter, 'O' (nasal), meaning, an Eye. *Position of Hebrew letter in alphabet*: Sixteenth, or Sixteen (16). *Numerical Value of Hebrew letter*: 70 (Seventy). *Symbolic Meaning of Path*: "The Renovating Intelligence." *Occult Concept of Path*: The higher aspect of this Path is indicative of that creative, innate spiritual power of God existing within the individual. If this God-power actually manifests itself within the individual, that person becomes as a semi-divine being, partaking of both the nature of a man and a God. He or she knows their True Will, is exalted thereby, and begins the arduous process of liberating the world through the exercise of that True Will in the world of mankind. *Basal Attribute of the Path*: the Zodiacal Sign of Capricorn. *Tarot Attribution of Path*: Tarot Trump, Fifteen (XV) — The Devil.

• *Path Number on the Tree*: Twenty-Seven (**27**), connecting Netzach and Hod.

Path Name: Peh (Hebrew letter 'P'), meaning, Mouth. *Position of Hebrew letter in alphabet*: Seventeenth, or Seventeen (17). *Numerical Value of Hebrew letter*: 80 (Eighty). *Symbolic Meaning of Path*: "The Exciting Intelligence." *Occult Concept of Path*: This Path exhibits the correspondence of Mars by virtue of its Basal Attribute, and consequently of the Sephirah Geburah in general, but in a more mundane manner. That is, it represents raw force, which although destructive in nature, yet has an implication in terms of a higher aspect in that it leads to a position of exalted spiritual, psychic and magical power, by he or she who survives the test of its raw, destructive force. Additionally, in a purely mystical sense, it endows every being in existence with spirit and movement, thereby giving motion to all life. *Basal Attribute of the Path*: The planet Mars. *Tarot Attribution of Path*: Tarot Trump, Sixteen (XVI) — The Tower.

• *Path Number on the Tree*: Twenty-Eight (**28**), connecting Netzach and Yesod.

Path Name: Tzaddi (Hebrew letters 'Ts' or 'Tz'), meaning, a Hook, or a Fish Hook. *Position of Hebrew letter in alphabet*: Eighteenth, or Eighteen (18). *Numerical Value of Hebrew letter*: 90 (Ninety). *Symbolic Meaning of Path*: "The Natural Intelligence." *Occult Concept of Path*: The feminine aspects of both the Moon and Venus which correspond to the two Sephiroth so joined by this Path, indicate the feminine nature of this Path as well. Through its creative impulses of this Path, Creation throughout the natural world is perfected and made whole. *Basal Attribute of the Path*: the Zodiacal Sign of Aquarius, though an Air Sign, is attributed to this Path, owing to its Water-Bearer symbology. *Tarot Attribution of Path*: Tarot Trump, Seventeen (XVII) — The Star.

• *Path Number on the Tree*: Twenty-Nine (**29**), connecting Netzach and Malkuth.

Path Name: Qoph (Hebrew letter 'Q'), meaning, the Back of the Head. *Position of Hebrew letter in alphabet*: Nineteenth, or Nineteen (19). *Numerical Value of Hebrew letter*: 100 (One hundred). *Symbolic Meaning of Path*: "The Corporeal Intelligence." *Occult Concept of Path*: While there are a host of attributions and correspondences assigned to this Path, none of them truly explain its nature. My own metaphysical and magical investigations of this Path have shown it to be a type of channel in the Astral Light through which those spiritual, psychic, and material desires and wants of the individual are made manifest. Specifically, I am referring to those magical acts that are intended to produce an effect in the physical world. It does not matter what Sephirah the magician may be working with—the role of Yesod as the foundation for all manifestations of metaphysical, mystical, and magical work being taken into account, of course—it nevertheless appears that this Path is invoked automatically in translating those manifestations into physical form. It is a very powerful Path in this regard, and one that is all too often overlooked in magical work in particular, and in occult work in general. The meanings of the two Sephiroth involved, and this Path's effects, should be carefully studied by the modern occult and magical practitioner. *Basal Attribute of the Path*: the negative, or feminine, polarity: watery, Zodiacal Sign Pisces. *Tarot Attribution of Path*: Tarot Trump, Eighteen (XVIII) — The Moon. (Notice the watery, female, creative aspects of the card in reference to the *Occult Concept of the Path*. Also, the reader would do well to consider the Lunar nature of this card as being the Planetary Attribution of Yesod, and the characteristic of this Path as a channel for material manifestation, as explained above.)

• *Path Number on the Tree*: Thirty (**30**), connecting Hod and Yesod.

Path Name: Resh (Hebrew letter 'R'), meaning, a Head. *Position of Hebrew letter in alphabet*: Twentieth, or Twenty (20). *Numerical Value of Hebrew letter*: 200 (Two hundred). *Symbolic Meaning of Path*: "The Collecting Intelligence." *Occult Concept of Path*: All of the attributions of this Path are strictly solar. As such, they refer to the attributes and correspondences assigned to the Sephirah Tiphareth, and to its Sensible Qualities produced and governed by the Sun. It is therefore a Path that 'collects' the attributes of the Sun such as Light, Life, Love, and Growth of every type, as well as the attributes of Hod, and combines them with foundational characteristics of Yesod discussed earlier in preparation for bringing them down into Malkuth through the Thirty-Second Path. This part of the process of manifestation in Malkuth—here, through Path 30—occurs in a masculine, fiery, and dynamic way, owing to the solar forces involved, as contrasted to the watery, passive, feminine process used by the Path 28, Tzaddi (the Feminine, Passive nature of the Pillar of Severity of which Hod is a part notwithstanding). *Basal Attribute of the Path*: the First Planet of the Ancients, the Sun. *Tarot Attribution of Path*: Tarot Trump, Nineteen (XIX) — The Sun.

• *Path Number on the Tree*: Thirty-One (**31**), connecting Hod and Malkuth.

Path Name: Shin (Hebrew letter 'Sh'), meaning a Tooth. *Position of Hebrew letter in alphabet*: Twenty-First, or Twenty-One (21). *Numerical Value of Hebrew letter*: 300 (Three hundred). *Symbolic Meaning of Path*: "The Perpetual Intelligence." *Occult Concept of Path*: The fiery descent of Divine Wisdom and the dedication to live that state in the world of mankind. An example which conveys the principles behind such an awakening is found in the descent of the Holy Ghost upon the Apostles, enlightening them, and bringing about the resolve within each of them necessary to take the teachings of the Divine Christ to the people of the world, amidst the hostile Roman and Pagan forces that pressed upon them from every side. Recall also the *Occult Concept* of Path 30 as well, and its implication in this Hod-to-Yesod and Hod-to-Malkuth connection. *Basal Attribute of the Path*: the Element, Fire. *Tarot Attribution of Path*: Tarot Trump, Twenty (XX) — The Last Judgment.

• *Path Number on the Tree*: Thirty-Two (**32**), connecting Yesod and Malkuth.

Path Name: Tav (Hebrew letter 'T'), meaning, a Cross, and specifically a three-armed cross. That is, a cross shaped as the letter 'T.' *Position of Hebrew letter in alphabet*: Twenty-Second, or Twenty-Two (22). *Numerical Value of Hebrew letter*: 400 (Four hundred). *Symbolic Meaning of Path*: "The Administrative Intelligence." *Occult Concept of Path*: Besides the implication of the purpose of this 32nd Path given in the discussion for Path 30, Path 32 possesses a bittersweet characteristic, but only owing to the 'higher-minded' of the Kabbalists who translated such a bittersweet necessity as 'evil.' This 32nd Path is that portal or channel which allows the coarsest matter of the Astral Plane to enter the world of Malkuth, while also representing all existing intelligences throughout Creation at the same time. My personal experience of this Path has shown it to be, in reality, the Path that governs the mechanics of physical existence, which can be pointedly summed up as providing a common plane for the existence and expression of both good and evil, all at the same time. Thus, it is a stage wherein the drama of daily material, psychic, and spiritual life unfolds, grows, expands, interacts, and develops, with each of these facets of Creation set up according to its own rules and laws. *Basal Attribute of the Path*: The planet, Saturn. *Tarot Attribution of Path*: Tarot Trump, Twenty-One (XXI) — The World.

If the reader has paid careful attention to the Sephiroth and Path material, and has spent a reasonable length of time contemplating it, he or she now has an adequate base of knowledge from which to proceed; not only in learning the fundamental components of the Kabbalah, but in carefully and correctly building and strengthening their subconscious state of subjective synthesis. As you are also well aware, up to this point I have focused on the Intelligible Qualities of the Sephiroth and Paths, by providing the higher aspects of the Symbolic Meanings, always extrapolating the more practical or Sensible Qualities as if they were of secondary importance.

Again, I cannot emphasize too strongly, this was necessary to provide for your newly forming or expanding state of subjective synthesis, and for building up within you a realistic framework into which your more advanced Kabbalistic studies can be easily and effectively placed. Having belabored these points, we will finally focus exclusively on what underlies our special and pragmatic interests in 'working' magic: the *Sensible Qualities of both the Sephiroth and the Paths.*

If you will recall, I stated earlier that since each of the Sephiroth are Paths themselves, they possess a Sensible Quality by virtue of their Astrological Attribution or planetary correspondence. The Sensible Qualities of the Sephiroth are thus projected into the world of Malkuth through the projections radiating from these correspondences. I also posed the question that if this is the case, and all of the Seven Planets of the Ancients have already been assigned to Binah through Yesod, then where are the projectors of the remaining twenty-two Paths which project into the lower or more mundane World of Malkuth, as the Sephiroth did?

I further stated that there was only one important, fundamental correspondence of the *Sensible Qualities of the Paths,* and that fundamental correspondence is *the* attribution of the Paths that you will be using to work the Kabbalah on a practical basis. This is whether that basis is strictly in your *daily* magical work, or in your private, mundane life matters as well, should you choose to use the Kabbalah as a universal set from which to draw your inspiration and strength. You will find however, that that same single correspondence will also be the Key to your successful working of Path Magic.

As you may have guessed, *the fundamental attribution that projects the Sensible Qualities of the Paths into the World of Malkuth is the Tarot.* Neither the feminine nor masculine polarities of the Paths, the numerical values of the Hebrew letters, their placements in the Hebrew alphabet, nor their Symbolic Meanings, have anything to do with the use of the Kabbalah in your *daily, mundane life affairs*, should you choose to use the Kabbalah here, as I have given in *Kabbalistic Cycles and the Mastery of Life*.

They, along with their Basal Attribute, most certainly do play a central role in the working of magic in general, and that includes the working of Path Magic as previously mentioned. (In the latter case, these higher aspects of the Paths are used in advanced work when one wishes to explore the mystical basis of the Paths, and the higher aspects of the Sephiroth). I further caution the reader to take note of the term *daily life*, because as I said, these other attributions do and most certainly **will** have a great deal of importance in your understanding, comprehending, and apprehending the Kabbalah proper, *and*—once more—**will** most certainly be of use to you in *advanced* magical work and Kabbalistic Analyses.

I have not contradicted myself here in terms of what has just been written in the last paragraph. Please reread the above paragraph and this one carefully, and I think you will see the thin line of distinction I am trying to make clear in these matters. Repetition is the basis of all long term learning. So to repeat myself once more, it is your overall knowledge of the Kabbalah that will enable you to use this theological system effectively and efficiently in your daily life should you so choose to employ it there, in addition to applying it constantly to your magical practices.

In reality, all parts not only support the whole, but go into making it up as well. It is simply that we *typically* use the Tarot and the planetary projections of the Sephiroth to apply the Kabbalah in general terms to our daily magical practices and worldly affairs. Since you now know the planetary attributions of the Sephiroth, we will turn to an exposition of the Paths' Tarot correspondences, so that the full effects of the Kabbalah can become a living part of your subjective synthesis.

Chapter Six

Concerning The Tarot, Its Path Assignments, and Path Working Magic

Although the Tarot is chiefly used as a divinatory tool in daily life by casting a spread, we have a higher purpose for it. The higher purpose is as a means of gaining access to the magical energy of the Path to which each of the twenty-two Cards of the Greater Arcana is assigned. Having accessed this energy, we can then:

1. Direct it to fulfill some material purpose—as we will be using the energy from its Sensible Qualities, or we can—
2. Use it to propel ourselves into either Sephiroth, one at a time, connected by any given Path, for the purpose of exploring the Intelligible Qualities of a given Sephirah. (Some will insist on referring to this exploration activity as a means of 'increasing their spiritual growth.' Actually, it stimulates one's intellectual growth, emotional appreciation for the obvious and subtle beauties of life and Creation, and for developing the psychic faculties tremendously. As a further aside, the reader should carefully consider that the Spiritual Nature within each individual is already perfect. The One could not have made it any other way when placing a Part of Itself into the human psyche.)

We begin this process by mastering two relatively simple things:

1. Developing a relatively quick understanding and comprehension of the Sensible Qualities *only*, that the cards are said to 'project' or stand for according to tradition, and—
2. Confining ourselves to using only the twenty-two cards of the Greater Arcana or the Trumps Major, as opposed to the addi-

143

tional fifty-six cards of the Lesser Arcana; that is, the four Suits or fourteen cards each.

Why do we first concern ourselves with the Sensible Qualities of the Tarot as they are assigned to the Paths, and only later deal with their Intelligible Qualities in Path Working Magic? Because despite the fanciful view engendered by christianized Western thinking and its extension—the New Age phenomenon—we are not 'spiritual beings' who are dominated by our divine natures. It is not the 'spiritual' impulse that is the dominant force in our mundane—nor magical—life.

The hard and straight fact of the matter is that we are physical beings with physical reference points, feelings, needs, wants, and emotions, all of which act as filters through which—at best—we distortedly see the world around us. Put bluntly, we are beings driven by the five physical senses, and as a result, *know* those physical concepts that fall under the heading of "Sensible Qualities" better than we do the oft touted 'spiritual' or Intelligible Qualities. The reader may not like to hear this, but that does not change the way things are.

Thus, by beginning with the Sensible Qualities, and only later extending our awareness into the abstractions of the Intelligible Qualities of a given Path, can we come to fully and completely apprehend both its Sensible and Intelligible Qualities in order to harness the magical energy of the Path, and the Sephiroth it connects. This is why we begin with the Sensible. It is where we are at.

Now, I can hear some of my readers' objections at this point. You may wonder how I 'legitimize' such a view and procedure? You may feel this is some contrivance to 'make' this technique work. Certainly, you think you should be concerned with the exalted 'spiritual' or Intelligible Qualities first, and then work backwards. That is, work downward, until you reach the Sensible Qualities behind the cards. Well, to prove to you this is not some contrivance on my part, but rather, a technique I developed throughout many long years of experimenting, allow me to explain further.

First off, it is as I said. Face the facts. It is where we as a species are at this moment in history. Remember too, that as with the Sephiroth and Paths, it was necessary for you to gain a foundational understanding of their attributes and correspondences, so you could begin to understand and appreciate the intricacies and beauties of Kabbalah. By these, I mean the Intelligible Qualities underlying this theological system of thought. And how did you begin? What (no doubt) was easier for you to immediately relate to? Of course, it was the Sensible Qualities of those Sephiroth and Paths.

Remember also I cautioned that the state of your subjective synthesis, which is the extent of the superstructure you erect on this foundational knowledge, will determine how effectively and efficiently your magic will work. And to effect this, you have to begin where you are at. Right now. Right here. Not somewhere you pretend to be or want to be in your overall development. Thus, the information I gave you on the Sephiroth and the Paths was more than sufficient for you to either strengthen your state of subjective synthesis, or to begin building it up from scratch. And the manner in which I delivered it to you should take you over the top to establish a state of subjective synthesis that is second to none. Now your magic will work that much more effectively and efficiently, starting almost immediately, as you will soon realize for yourself.

So you see, it was not just giving you the knowledge of the Kabbalah that was important, as vitally important as that knowledge is. It was the *method of delivery* which I trust enabled you to grasp, comprehend, and (eventually) apprehend its meaning and connections to your daily and magical life, while at the same time, perceiving the sublime beauty of this special theosophy. This is a beauty that can only enable you to grow and prosper as an enlightened human being.

Of course, if—in this instance—you are serious about expanding your understanding of the Tarot, you will take my advice to heart, and also study a book I recommend—*The Pictorial Key to the Tarot*, written by Arthur Edward Waite.[25] This book explains clearly both the Intelligible and Sensible attributions of the cards in a highly detailed and insightful way. But most importantly, in this hallmark contribution, Waite's mystical insights of each of the cards of the Greater Arcana will grant you insight into the Intelligible Qualities you most certainly will need in your later Path Working magical work.

(Please note, even though Waite's work is complete, I also strongly recommend the following, but only for those who wish to penetrate further into the study and understanding of this fascinating magical energy device—the Tarot—as I prefer to think of this collection of 78 cards. They are: *The Tarot: Its Occult Significance, Use in Fortune-Telling, and Method of Play*, by S.L. MacGregor Mathers,[26] and *The Magical Ritual of the Sanctum Regnum, Interpreted by the Tarot Trumps*, by Eliphas Levi, and translated by W. Wynn Westcott.[27])

By using what is provided in this book, and expanding upon it with Waite's work as your primary outside study text, and contemplating the Intelligible and Sensible meanings assigned to the twenty-two cards of the Greater Arcana by virtue of their symbolism, you will eventually reach that same state of apprehension of the Tarot as you reached in your mastery of the Kabbalistic Sephiroth and Paths. Then you will possess it all. But for now, to enable you to begin your investigations into Path Working Magic, only the mastery of the Sensible Qualities of the cards is necessary. *That is, those that you will find in this chapter*. This will at least give you insights into the mundane characteristics of the cards, and provide a base for your later study of the Intelligible qualities Waite so admirably delves into.

Thus, Path Working Magic as presented here, is a piece-wise process. As with so many things in life, this type of magic is not something you flippantly jump into. It is a *process*, the elements of which must first be understood and then properly applied, before benefit can be reaped. As you will soon see, the technique presented here for achieving this is not one that uses ritual techniques. Rather, it is a method grounded in mystical contemplation. Not 'dynamic' enough for *you*, the practicing magician? Only you, the reader, will be able to answer that question after having learned the technique presented here, and after having given it a fair run. But I am willing to bet I know what your answer will be!

Secondly, I did not assign the twenty-two cards of the Greater Arcana to the twenty-two Paths of the Tree of Life. These were assigned to the Paths by the creators of the Kabbalah and its later students. Of course, they paid special attention to the Sensible Qualities, and for the obvious reasons I delineated above. Thus, you can legitimately concern yourself with this limited Arcana only.

Since the reader is being introduced to a new technique for Path Working Magic, it is necessary to build upon what has gone before, and upon each new level, add yet another. This procedure necessitates that we first explore the Sensible Qualities of the twenty-two cards of the Greater Arcana in a comprehensive and logical manner. Please be certain to refer to Figure 4 throughout the discussion to follow. It will help you to understand, and enable you to quickly become acquainted with the position of the Tarot Trumps on the Paths. Of course, you should also have in your possession the Rider-Waite Tarot deck, and view each card as they are discussed herein. Remember too, that these mundane or Sensible Qualities, as I term them, are just that. They are brief, mundane characteristics that I and many, many others have found to hold true for these cards: both in casting a spread, and most importantly, for their use in Path Working Magic.

Lastly, you will see meanings given for each card in both its 'upright' position and its 'reversed' or 'upside down' position. That is, in the upright position, the figures on the card are in a normal position, and the card number—for example, the card, The Fool (0)—points outward and away from you. In the reversed or upside down position, the picture literally appears upside down or reversed, and the card number—as with the example of The Fool—points inward and toward you. The meanings of the two positions of each card must first be memorized and then studied and contemplated. Why give different positioning for each card? In my book on Kabbalistic Cycles, the positioning had one purpose. Here, it has another. Specifically, it is given here as an added 'plus.' That is, when you involve yourself in using the Tarot for divinatory purposes only, you will have at your command an immediate reference to enable you to understand what the cards mean when they are in the upright or 'reversed' position, which in turn will aid you in arriving at an accurate interpretation of a spread.

Now, what is this so called 'new' technique for practicing Path Working Magic all about? First off, let me say, that there is a not so old magical maxim that—if I recall correctly—was first uttered by Brodie-Innes, after the breakup of the original Golden Dawn Temple in 1900: 'In the end, we all become Mystics.' The wedding of Magic and Mysticism is not something new in and of itself, as any working magician knows. The practices of Imaging (what some call Visualization) and Concentration are mystically-based activities in their own right. That is, when Mysticism is viewed as an inner process, designed to open and develop some inner psychic function or to access some higher spiritual quality.

As the magician proceeds further on their own self-stylized magical path, they will find much truth in this view. They will also find that the line of division between Magic and Mysticism becomes more clearly defined, until a choice finally has to be made between the two. Impossible you say? You probably contend that you are a magician and always will be, and that I don't know what I am talking about. Well, we will see.

Indeed, the *experimental* magician will face this dilemma at some point in his or her career. As to the theoretical magician facing such a quandary? It will never happen, for the latter lacks the *experiential knowledge* that precipitates this personal *spiritual*— yes, *'spiritual'* crisis—because in this single instance, the *source of the crisis is the perfected spiritual nature within the individual.* Just a little something for the curious reader to think about. That being said, we can now look at this new Path Working technique in detail.

The Mystical Technique of Path Working Magic

In the Preface to the classic book of mystical instruction, *The Spiritual Exercises of Saint Ignatius, or the Manresa*,[28] the interested student can find a concise review of a mystical process that—as you might expect—is geared toward the Catholic doctrinal view of Christ, and of attaining what that church conceives of as a state of 'true' discipleship with Him. Nevertheless, the instructions are so well founded and insightful, that the magician need only replace—if he or she chooses—the words 'Jesus Christ' or 'Christ' with some other spiritual term of their own choosing, while eliminating all references to 'Holy Mother Church.' In fact, while not openly admitted, this book has served as the basis of many magician's practical Ascent to the Mountain Top, not the least of which included my old friend and mentor, Francis Israel Regardie. It is this approach that we use in performing effective Path Working Magic.

In point of fact, while reading the text, the contemporary magician will wonder if Ignatius is not preparing the reader for the Abramelin Operation designed to Attain to the Knowledge and Conversation of the Holy Guardian Angel (K&C of the HGA)!

For here, Ignatius discusses the obstacles that must be overcome in experiencing the chief powers of the soul. Namely: the attainment and maintenance of silence and solitude; the cessation of ordinary business and study; the elimination of all reading that is foreign to the exercises he prescribes; the elimination of all thoughts that are not in harmony with the Work being undertaken; self-mortification (in the sense of abstinence from physical pleasures); and prayer, to name but a few of the conditions required of the student to "...use the faculties of their understanding and their heart."[29]

But it is in this Saint's practical instruction for the attainment of the psychic state that follows from such rigor—and which eventually does lead one to contact their truly spiritual nature—that we find a *precise* magical parallel (dogmatic nonsense aside) that can be used in our exploration of the Paths of the Holy Tree of Life, and in the acquisition of the magical energy those Paths contain. For it is in the first paragraph of Ignatius' Introduction that he tells us that which we want to know (for the sake of completeness and further discussion, I am quoting from the *Manresa* exactly as it is given. Any readers finding offense with the use of the words 'Jesus Christ,' or 'the Commandments,' or 'the church,' within some of the following quotations, must remember the context of Ignatius' work):

"By *Spiritual Exercises* is understood certain operations of the mind and heart, such as the examination of conscience, meditation, contemplation, mental and vocal prayer, which are employed in order to free the soul from its irregular affections, and so to put it in the way of knowing and embracing the will of God towards it."[30]

While he does continue on throughout the book to give specific details of these processes (and which the earnest reader would do well to study carefully) it is in the above simple exhortation that we find the keys for effective Path Working Magic. Namely,

- Examination
- Meditation
- Contemplation

Of *Examination*, the *Manresa* then counsels, "When the attentive soul looks in upon itself, in order to compare its thoughts, its words, its actions, with the commandments of God and the Church, to sigh over the opposition which it finds between its conduct and the Divine law, this exercise is called "Examination," and is either general or particular, according as it refers to all the faults committed, or to only one kind,—*quotidien*, or that which is made every day, or that which is preparatory to ordinary or extraordinary confession."[31]

The unknown writer of the Preface in which the above is found further states, "St. Ignatius recommends this exercise above all others, as without doubt the most conducive to a knowledge and reform of ourselves, the most favorable to reflection, and the least likely to lead to exaltation and enthusiasm."[31]

Of *Meditation*, our prefacer writes, "When the memory has recalled to the soul the recollection of some dogmatical or moral truth, when the understanding exerts itself to penetrate it, and the will to submit to it, attach and devote itself to it, we then say that we meditate. Meditation is also called the 'Exercise of the three Powers of the Soul.'"[32]

Regarding Contemplation, we find in the Preface, "In this age, so little contemplative, we must define exactly what is meant by contemplation. We contemplate rather than meditate when, after the memory has recalled the whole, or some detail, of the life of our Lord Jesus Christ, the soul, in a state of profound recollection, employs itself in seeing, hearing, considering the different circumstances of the mystery, for the purpose of being instructed, edified, and moved by it. This contemplation takes the name of "Application of the Senses" when the soul nourishes itself at leisure, and without the employment of the understanding, on all that the mystery offers to it to see, to hear, to taste, to feel, almost as if the fact present to the imagination passed before the eyes, and affected all bodily senses. Thus, in meditation, it is the *understanding* which is exerted on an abstract truth, of which it seeks to be convinced; in *contemplation*, it is the soul that applies itself to the Incarnate Truth..."[33]

How do we use Ignatius' basic instruction set, to practice Path Working Magic, contact the magical energy there, and direct it at our own discretion? The answer—and the process—is actually quite simple.

• First, we begin with the Sensible Qualities of the Tarot cards as previously explained. (Remember: it is primarily through the cards that the Path energies find their way into Malkuth, and it is the cards that *express the nature of the energy of a given Path*.) We **initially** apply the processes of Examination, Meditation, and Contemplation to the more mundane attributes of the cards, as found in this chapter, and **later** expand those same processes to the Intelligible Qualities of the Paths—that are also expressed by the cards—which Waite so admirably covers in his classic text.

• Second, as Ignatius counsels, "When the attentive soul looks in upon itself, in order to compare its thoughts, its words, its actions…to sigh over the opposition which it finds between its conduct and the Divine law…this exercise is called 'Examination' …"

How do we apply this exhortation in Path Working Magic? We study a specific card in detail until we know its features and Sensible Qualities (at first) thoroughly, and then internalize its graphical depiction and those qualities. We do not see the card—and hence the energy of the Path it represents—as existing outside of us, but rather, as a living aspect that dwells deep within our very nature. **And of course, a Kabbalistic Analysis is absolutely necessary to accomplish this.** In effect, when we do this, we begin to make contact with the energy of the Path represented by the card in question, through a type of 'psychic sympathy.' We *emotionally feel* the meanings behind the card—and hence of the Path—*after* our mental effort to learn and understand it.

• Third. "When the memory has recalled to the soul the recollection of some dogmatical or moral truth, when the understanding exerts itself to penetrate it, and the will to submit to it, attach and devote itself to it, we then say that we meditate."

In other words, unlike the everyday process of first intellectualizing a matter and then allowing the emotions to react to it, in Ignatius' Meditation we *intellectualize the insights*—whether of the Sensible or Intelligible Qualities—of a card, *after* having experienced an emotional reaction to it through the process of Examination. Our task in the meditative state then becomes one of using the Will to unite the emotional reaction to the intellectual understanding we have of the Path. This creates a type of conducting link between the magical energy of the Path and our state of Subjective Synthesis, and produces a very curious conscious mental feeling—akin to a powerful alteration in consciousness that lasts for many hours or even days, depending upon the individual and upon the depth of the insights achieved when the link is first forged.

• In the fourth and final step of the process, "We contemplate rather than meditate when, after the memory has recalled the whole, or some detail...the soul, in a state of profound recollection, employs itself in seeing, hearing, considering the different circumstances of the mystery, for the purpose of being instructed, edified, and moved by it. This contemplation takes the name of 'Application of the Senses' when the soul nourishes itself at leisure, and without the employment of the understanding, on all that the mystery offers to it to see, to hear, to taste, to feel, almost as if the fact present to the imagination passed before the eyes, and affected all bodily senses. Thus, in meditation, it is the *understanding* which is exerted on an abstract truth, of which it seeks to be convinced; in *contemplation*, it is the soul that applies itself to the Incarnate Truth..."

In this final step, the intellectual nature is abandoned. Contemplation of the abstract behind the symbols of the cards, and of their sensible meanings, occurs through an emptying of the mind of all but an awareness of the symbolism and meaning of the cards, but without conscious straining. This is much like simply looking at a picture while in a daydream state. This induces the "Application of the Senses," *wherein the meanings and energy of the cards actually enter into Malkuth,* having made their way 'downward' into the sense. That is, into the physical, bodily organs of the magician which, of course, are his immediate and predominant connections with Malkuth, and thus with the physical side of life he or she so desires to effect by directing the magical energy of a given Path.

How can this be? The first step of the process, Examination, activates the emotions, which, in turn, stimulates the mind into an intellectualized understanding of the Path and its power through Meditation. Contemplation is that action that welds the energy of the Path to the physical world of the magician. Kabbalistically interpreted, the energy and power of the Paths exist as pure abstractions, highly charged with a conscious, living energy, in Atziluth. Examination brings them down into Briah, the creative world, where through Meditation, the mind operates upon them, and they upon the mind and soul of the magician.

From here they are passed down into Yetzirah, the World of Formation where—through the final act of the process of Concentration—the "Application of the Senses" occur. It is through this final act in which the insights and abstractions are physically felt in the body of the magician, that the energy is linked to the physical world of Assiah—the world of action—in which the magician truly lives, moves, and has his being.

It's as simple as that. Now. How do we:

1. Direct the energy of a given Path into our magical and worldly activities? (The following example will only be for the direction of a Path's energy into a mundane matter, since, at first, you will only be working with the energy of the Sensible Quality. The latter application of the energy to the higher aspects of the Path are up to the individual magician to discover for themselves. That is what magic is all about—or should be: *self discovery through personal experimentation.*)

2. Use this energy to explore the nature and forces of a given Sephirah connected by the Path?

In the first instance, after the symbolism of a given card has been Examined, that is, a Kabbalistic Analysis has been performed on it and it has been internalized by our having experienced a psychic sympathy with its symbolism through a deep emotional reaction to it, we use our Will to wed our intellectual understanding of that symbolism to our emotional reaction to it in Meditation. When this happens, a type of 'energized enthusiasm' will be felt in the mind. But here is where the critically different magical part of the process enters.

Prior to emptying the mind in Contemplation, we identify the card in question with some sensible (material) end we wish to effect or achieve through the use of the Path's energy. That is, we focus on the card, projecting our specific desire upon it, and then—*and only then*—we Contemplate the card by emptying our mind of all but an awareness of its symbolism and meaning. When this happens, the energy of the Path is transferred through the card to that desire, through our state of subjective synthesis. That is, the energy is transferred through the medium of our subconscious (or unconscious) mind.

Then, physical sensations will arise within the body of the magician, a sign that the energized desire has been brought down into the world of Malkuth. In short, when this final state of physical sensation is reached, the energy of the Path will have found its way into Malkuth, and the desire that has been projected onto the card will manifest in the world of matter. Now you know how to perform Path Working Magic in a way that will most certainly work for you. It has been tested and retested by myself, and by more people than I can count to whom I have taught it. And it works.

If all of this sounds like a type of New Age 'fad magic' that I am so set against, remember: the basis for it lies in the aged traditional writing of Saint Ignatius, and in the ancient mystical doctrines of Kabbalah. In point of fact then, this technique is about as far from New Age techniques as I am.

As for using the Tarot as a backdoor method to explore the nature and forces of a given Sephirah connected by a given Path, the process differs significantly in several respects, and is much more complicated. Yet it produces amazing results and is worth the effort as you will find, should you dare to enter into this particular form of High Magic practice.

A Sephirotic Invocation Ritual of the Sephirah in question is first performed, using the splendid and precise methods given in Mr. Griffin's book, *The Ritual Magic Manual*.[7] As will be found by studying the appropriate section of Mr. Griffin's book, the magician will eventually reach the point in the ritual performance where they state their magical intentions for performing the ritual, such as, "I am performing this rite to penetrate into the nature and energy of the Sephirah (for example) Hod."

At this point, the magician sits down and, while fixing their gaze upon the Tarot card leading to this Sephirah, performs the Examination and the Meditation as discussed earlier. When the state of energized enthusiasm is reached, he or she does not project a mundane or material desire onto the card. Rather, the magician slips into the state of Contemplation. Here, when the mind is emptied of all but an awareness of the symbolism and meaning of the card, something very abrupt will happen. The physical sensations will automatically begin to arise in the body, and the magician will find themselves hurled into a different world of visual and sensory experience. This is the realm of the Sephirah itself.

This experience will be so far beyond that achieved in Scrying or Spirit Vision or even exploring the 30 Aethyrs of the Enochian system of magic, as to make the individual realize they have no point of reference in this strange, new, and powerful world. It is during this time that the magician can explore either the mundane, Sensible Qualities of the Sephirah, or those exalted Intelligible Qualities of abstraction the Sphere symbolizes.

In the latter case, it will take a great deal of time and practice to be able to 'return' with the insights into the abstractions received, as this mystical process of exploration does not lend itself well to translation into the mundane world of form. That is, it is like trying to mix oil and water, two substances that are immiscible with each other. For this reason, the magician should immediately write down the visions and impressions received upon returning from their exalted mental state to an awareness of the Temple and the ritual area, before completing and closing the ritual part of the Operation as is so beautifully given in *The Ritual Magic Manual*.

An exposition of the Tarot Trumps now follows. Please reread and think this chapter through carefully. You will find it to be a very effective addition to your magical treasure chest of wish-fulfillment and ritual techniques.

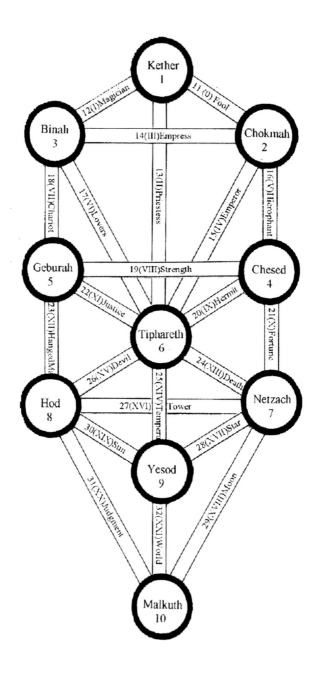

Figure 4. The Tree of Life. Glyph 2.

The Fool (0)

Corresponding Path on the Tree: Number 11 (Eleven)—Aleph—Connecting Kether and Chokmah. *Sensible Meaning in Malkuth*. In the *upright* position: Foolhardiness in action; foolishness in thought and deed; wildly excessive behavior; extravagant behavior, thoughts, and propositions. A greatly exaggerated sense of one's own importance and position in life; fantastic ideas and speculations. In the *reversed* position: trouble stemming from the extravagances listed above. Also difficulties from indecision, vacillation, and irresolution.

The Magician (I)

Corresponding Path on the Tree: Number 12 (Twelve)—Beth—Connecting Kether and Binah. *Sensible Meaning in Malkuth*. In the *upright* position: power of the individual's resolve; appropriate skills to meet the task at hand; power of the will to effect the change desired; confidence in one's own ideas, abilities, and the determination to carry them through to completion. In the *reversed* position: conceit; lack of appropriate skills for the task at hand; lack of self confidence; lack of will to effect the change(s) sought; lack of individual power and resolve to effect the ends desired.

The High Priestess (II)

Corresponding Path on the Tree: Number 13 (Thirteen)—Gimel—Connecting Kether and Tiphareth. *Sensible Meaning in Malkuth*. In the *upright* position: knowledge; deep thought; scientific thought, ideas, and all matters pertaining to scientific education. Also, educational matters in general. Logical thought; rational thinking and cogent argument style; cognitive skills. In the *reversed* position: illiteracy; ignorance; shallowness of thought and idea; surface knowledge; a lack of structure of the knowledge one is seeking.

The Empress (III)

Corresponding Path on the Tree: Number 14 (Fourteen)—Daleth—Connecting Chokmah and Binah. *Sensible Meaning in Malkuth*. In the *upright* position: fecundity in all matters, prolific results; accomplishment; the act of doing, fruitfulness in all things; earthiness; creativity. In the *reversed* position: dissipation of one's energy; loss of power in general; incomplete results due to hesitancy, indecision, or irresolution in acting.

The Emperor (IV)

Corresponding Path on the Tree: Number 15 (Fifteen)—Heh—Connecting Chokmah and Tiphareth. *Sensible Meaning in Malkuth.* In the *upright* position: one's right or prerogative to rule or to determine for one's self; authority; command; control; domination; effective action; mastery; might; the power of reason; justification; the making of rationalizations that are right and just. In the *reversed* position: juvenile, childish emotions and their display; loss of authority, control, and command. Blocked plans and schemes.

The Hierophant (V)

Corresponding Path on the Tree: Number 16 (Sixteen)—Vav—Connecting Chokmah and Chesed. *Sensible Meaning in Malkuth.* In the *upright* position: kindness; mercy; righteousness; morality; virtue; the quality of goodness; a person who exhibits these high human qualities. In the *reversed* position: excessive kindness; excessive mercy; weakness resulting from such excess; the inability to discern such excess, due to a lack of emotional control.

The Lovers (VI)

Corresponding Path on the Tree: Number 17 (Seventeen)—Zayin—Connecting Binah and Tiphareth. *Sensible Meaning in Malkuth.* In the *upright* position: a trial in life or an experiment of a personal nature that you will successfully conclude; the emergence of a new affection or object of devotion, whether it be a person or new interest of some type. In the *reversed* position: a failed life-trial or experiment; the loss of affection for a person or interest.

The Chariot (VII)

Corresponding Path on the Tree: Number 18 (Eighteen)—Cheth—Connecting Binah and Geburah. *Sensible Meaning in Malkuth.* In the *upright* position: victory, conquest, overcoming odds and obstructions, but only after battle. In the *reversed* position: defeat after battle; obstructions to plans and actions; plans and actions defeated by either internal or external obstructions and obstacles, but once again, only after battle. *Commentary*: this card, and card XVI—The Tower, Path 27, Peh—are the most difficult cards of the Greater Arcana. With either card, the plans made, the opportunities that arise, and the actions taken under their influence, have an extremely grim, major component to them. Of the two cards however, this card (VII) The Chariot, is perhaps surprisingly the hardest of the two to work with, even in its upright position, for it bespeaks of a long, arduous struggle which will take a heavy toll on the individual, even though he or she will become victorious (when it is in the upright position).

Strength (VIII)

Corresponding Path on the Tree: Number 19 (Nineteen)—Teth—Connecting Chesed and Geburah. *Sensible Meaning in Malkuth*. In the *upright* position: metaphysical or spiritual force and strength; inner strength which overcomes danger and adversity. The strength through which the Holy warrior battles against overwhelming odds, and victoriously subdues and overcomes a great threat. Subjugation of opposition through spiritual power. In the *reversed* position: power and strength, but physical in nature. Endurance and determination in matters requiring physical strength, and the physical prowess through which these qualities are sustained.

The Hermit (IX)

Corresponding Path on the Tree: Number 20 (Twenty)—Yod—Connecting Chesed and Tiphareth. *Sensible Meaning in Malkuth*. In the *upright* position: deliberation, due to watchful attention, or a feeling of caution; a warning, things are not as they seem. Also, the furthering of psychic growth. In the *reversed* position: excessive self-admonition or over cautiousness in important matters; imprudent actions; ill-advised activities; indiscreet behavior.

The Wheel of Fortune (X)

Corresponding Path on the Tree: Number 21 (Twenty-one)—Kaph—Connecting Chesed and Netzach. *Sensible Meaning in Malkuth*. In the *upright* position: beneficence; expansiveness; growth; money; good luck; good fortune; success. In the *reversed* position: ill fortune; the reversal of dame fortune; hardship; loss; contraction; struggle; failure.

Justice (XI)

Corresponding Path on the Tree: Number 22 (Twenty-two)—Lamed—Connecting Geburah and Tiphareth. *Sensible Meaning in Malkuth*. In the *upright* position: harmony, justice, stability; poise; equilibrium; balance. In the *reversed* position: conflict, injustice; instability; imbalance, intolerance.

The Hanged Man (XII)

Corresponding Path on the Tree: Number 23 (Twenty-three)—Mem—Connecting Geburah and Hod. *Sensible Meaning in Malkuth*. In the *upright* position: the acquisition of knowledge which eventually matures into wisdom. The process is slow however, and as with life in general, requires sacrifices on the part of the individual for that knowledge to ripen into wisdom. In the *reversed* position: self-centeredness; concern for one's self exclusively at the obvious expense of others; sly, deceptive behavior designed to have one accepted by the group or masses.

Death (XIII)

Corresponding Path on the Tree: Number 24 (Twenty-four)—Nun—Connecting Tiphareth and Netzach. *Sensible Meaning in Malkuth*. In the *upright* position: physical death; an end; a massive, nebulous change or transformation in the individual, comparable to the end of a part of the self as occurs—for example—in the Attainment of the K&C of the HGA. In the *reversed* position: corruption; disintegration; decomposition through putrefaction; stasis. *Commentary:* this Path is not as difficult as it sounds. In reality, its meanings usually refer to the evolution and development of the Self through the process of self-growth, the means used to achieve this state notwithstanding. It is a hard path in terms of process, but its end results are stunning and utterly glorious.

Temperance (XIV)

Corresponding Path on the Tree: Number 25 (Twenty-five)—Samech—Connecting Tiphareth and Yesod. *Sensible Meaning in Malkuth*. In the *upright* position: to unite or wed seemingly disparate concepts, ideas, or actions in a positive and beneficial way; the use of temperate or measurable means and ways in thoughts and actions; a balanced approach to a problem, and the judicious implementation of its solution. In the *reversed* position: disparate concepts, ideas, or actions which cannot be conjoined or united; disagreement; loggerheads; an extreme approach to a problem and its unbalanced implementation, which not only does not resolve the original problem, but which creates additional problems as a result of the extreme measures employed.

The Devil (XV)

Corresponding Path on the Tree: Number 26 (Twenty-six)—Ayin—Connecting Tiphareth and Hod. *Sensible Meaning in Malkuth*. In the *upright* position: an eventual beneficial or favorable result arises from a seemingly deleterious event or situation. In the *reversed* position: that same situation produces an unfavorable or very unsatisfactory result, or is concluded in some negative and possibly harmful manner.

The Tower (XVI)

Corresponding Path on the Tree: Number 27 (Twenty-seven)—Peh—Connecting Netzach and Hod. *Sensible Meaning in Malkuth*. In the *upright* position: devolution; downfall; degeneration; decadence; disaster; calamity; tragedy; woes; catastrophe, disruption. In the *reversed* position: the same, but to a lesser degree. *Commentary*: this card, and card VII—The Chariot—along with their Paths, are by far the most difficult and dangerous Paths on the Tree as previously mentioned. Their influence is to be explored carefully at all times, and dealt with in an extremely cautious manner.

The Star (XVII)

Corresponding Path on the Tree: Number 28 (Twenty-eight)—Tzaddi—Connecting Netzach and Yesod. *Sensible Meaning in Malkuth*. In the *upright* position: happy expectation; joyful expectancy; happy prospects; an exciting future filled with many possibilities. In the *reversed* position: happy expectations and joyful expectancies are disappointed or thwarted; emptiness; effeteness.

The Moon (XVIII)

Corresponding Path on the Tree: Number 29 (Twenty-nine)—Qoph—Connecting Netzach and Malkuth. *Sensible Meaning in Malkuth*. In the *upright* position: secret enemies; cunning on the part of others for their own ends; deceit; duplicity; concealed forces in operation; hidden enemies; conspiracies against the individual innocently involved in a matter or situation. In the *reversed* position: the same, but to a lesser extent.

The Sun (XIX)

Corresponding Path on the Tree: Number 30 (Thirty)—Resh—Connecting Hod and Yesod. *Sensible Meaning in Malkuth.* In the *upright* position: bliss; happiness; contentment; joy; desires and goals achieved; wants satisfied; appeasement in general. In the *reversed* position: the same, but to a lesser extent.

The Last Judgment (XX)

Corresponding Path on the Tree: Number 31 (Thirty-one)—Shin—Connecting Hod and Malkuth. *Sensible Meaning in Malkuth.* In the *upright* position: rejuvenation; renewals of all types; outcomes reached; new beginnings; fresh starts. In the *reversed* position: problems causing efforts to bog down; delays; reversals; cowardly behavior.

The World (XXI)

Corresponding Path on the Tree: Number 32 (Thirty-two)—Tav—Connecting Yesod and Malkuth. *Sensible Meaning in Malkuth.* In the *upright* position: completion; assured success; compensation; remuneration; repayment; recompense; a prosperous or thriving conclusion. In the *reversed* position: stagnation, inertia; stasis; failed project or attempt; failure as a force, in general.

You now have the essential Sensible Qualities behind the cards that reflect the energy of the Paths to which they are assigned. Additionally, you now possess a unique, effective, and powerful method by which you can gain access to that energy. While the decision to involve yourself in Path Working Magic is completely up to the reader, I urge the individual to carefully consider experimenting with it. If this is done, you will no doubt add this relatively new area of magic to your arsenal of magical activities.

In so doing, you will expand your personal sphere of magical influence, and broaden your intellectual and conceptual understanding of the most powerful forces underlying the effective practice of magic—the Kabbalistic forces that underlie Creation itself. Finally, by adding this branch of magic to your personal, harmoniously balanced eclectic system of development, you will be strengthening your state of subjective synthesis greatly.

You will find as you continue to study and diligently experiment in magic, that the parts do indeed support and enhance the whole. This means that as your state of subjective synthesis is expanded, the expertise you gain in any given branch of magic will support and enhance the results you receive in another area of magical pursuit. Think this over well and decide. You have much to gain by carefully considering your involvement in Path Working Magic—and indeed, much to lose if you flippantly disregard the idea, looking only to the more commonly known and advertised forms of magic, such as Invocation and Evocation to Physical Manifestation.

Most assuredly, they have their places too, and so very important are the places that they occupy. But also remember what I cautioned concerning the parts supporting the whole. As in any diligent pursuit, all must be considered. For the old Welsh saying will truly ring in your ears at some later point in your magical life: "At the end of the day, you lay in the bed you make." It is up to you to determine just what type of bed that will be, and of the rest that will follow.

Chapter Seven

Concerning the Paraphernalia of Our Kabbalistic Art and Science

Preliminary Remarks

Every practitioner of magic knows from hard experience the difficulties in finding that certain suffumigation or 'incense' or metal, colored object, material, or any number of ritual and ceremonial 'secondary' requirements that turn out to be more demanding than first realized—at least in a time-wise sense. As the experimental magician also knows only too well, there are countless books out there on the market today that give information on those obtuse items needed to successfully perform a given magical act.

And that is the problem. There are so many, and the information is so scattered throughout the voluminous writings, that it not only requires a major research effort to find what one is looking for, but it also necessitates a serious financial outlay, as well as a serious effort to obtain these various sources. I cannot count the number of times I have heard or said myself "How I wish there was one single encyclopedic source for all of these things, because this seemingly endless searching is driving me crazy and the expense is breaking me!"

Unfortunately for all of us, that single source is still forthcoming. I only wish I could put it all together here for you, so you could just get on with your real work—the work of magic. But I cannot. At least, not in this present book, which was written to introduce other topics and techniques. Instead, I have opted for the following.

In this final chapter, I have tried my best to present lists of information that—while offering the most common information generally needed in many different branches of magic—is nonetheless typically found scattered throughout numerous other volumes. This condensation may therefore prove valuable to the magician, when they find themselves deeply involved in preparing for a ritual or ceremony that is in itself more than demanding in terms of its overall performance.

But also, I have tried something in this matter that you will find unique. I have added a few Commentaries here and there that will lift the veil of secrecy in several very important matters, while clarifying others. If I have succeeded in helping the reader by doing this, then this work will be that much more meaningful, and my ultimate satisfaction will be in knowing that I assisted the practicing magician as much as is possible through the written word.

Finally, realize that since most materials are used in so many different areas or branches of magic, placing them under a specific heading of magic would do little good. For instance. The metals ascribed to the Seven Planets of the Ancients could be placed under the heading 'Talismanic Magic,' even though those same metals are also used in Astrological Magic and in Evocation to Physical Manifestation. To provide for this and to make the lists that much more accessible, I have therefore not categorized the materials to be given under any particular branch of magical pursuit. The lists now follow. Use them well, to your best advantage.

I. Planetary Correspondences Assigned to Metals

    † Saturn — Lead † — See Commentary 1
    † Jupiter — Tin † — See Commentary 2
    † Mars—Iron (or high grade Steel) — See Commentary 3
    † Sun — Gold † — See Commentary 4
    † Venus — Copper † See Commentary 5
    † Mercury — "Fixed Mercury" — See Commentary 6
    † Moon — Silver — See Commentary 7

Commentary 1 — When working with any metal (or indeed, any object that is to be devoted to a magical purpose) be certain that it is virgin. This means it must never have been previously used for any other purpose. In the case of lead, for example, one might think an easy way of acquiring the lead needed for, say, making a sigil, would be to buy lead fishing sinkers, melt them down, and pour the plate or disk needed, right? Wrong! Why? The lead was already used for a given purpose—to make the sinkers! Using it will result in either no results, or worse yet, a very negative result. Always think in terms of 'virginity,' because the forces you are working with are intelligent, and *they* most certainly will be thinking in terms of this condition, I assure you!

Commentary 2 — Obtaining this element seems to be a considerable problem for many practitioners today. Usually, they resort to buying a thin disk they would like to believe is made of tin, or go to some machine shop or hardware store and buy a piece of sheet metal which the machinist or sales clerk assures them is 'genuine tin,' or 'has tin in it.' Don't be deceived! Your best bet is to search occult supply houses for a plate or disk—or whatever your particular requirement might be—for the genuine thing. In fact, you will no doubt find the following URL (Universal Resource Locator) World Wide Web site address invaluable in your search for magical items. It is actually a list of magical suppliers that carry almost any item you may be able to think of, or can help you find exactly what you are looking for. Its exhaustive listing of the various branches of magic, mysticism, wicca, occultism, and other belief systems will surely allow you to find what you are looking for in most—if not virtually all—cases. This web site address is:

http://dir.webring.com/rw?d=Religion___Beliefs

Personally, being a practitioner of the Old System of magic (Medieval Magic) I do things the 'old fashioned way' straight across the board in all of the magical requirements set down in any of the branches of magic. In the case of working with metals, I purchase the metals raw, melt them down, and pour whatever object I need: be it a plate, medallion, disk, or other device used for a particular magical end. In the case of Tin (it usually comes in pellet form) I buy the element from a legitimate chemical supply house that guarantees a 99.9% purity. Indeed, there are many such places on the World Wide Web that offer 'virgin' metals, and a simple search always turns up at least a few suppliers from which I can obtain this or any other metal. It is expensive to do it this way, but again, the magical results are always so great, that personally I would never think of doing it any other way.

Commentary 3 — Iron, as a readily available, pure element, is not easy to come by in this age of the do-everything-for-me teckie. The first possibility here is to visit a jewelry store and ask for a stainless steel disk or small plate. I'm told it's a current fad to add 'common metal' to exorbitantly expensive charm bracelets, thereby giving the astute magician another source for the metal assigned to this planet. Be certain, however, that it is virgin, and that it is 'stainless' steel.

As for my own work, I have found that most chemical supply houses that do carry elemental iron generally sell it in the form of an oxide, sulfide, or sulfate, which is difficult to work with in order to extract the iron from the compound. But once again, being determined to fulfill ancient writ, I have found that there are a few places on the World Wide Web that do indeed sell iron in an easily workable granular form, and at extremely reasonable prices. As always, it is up to the serious magician to determine what is best in their own particular case, and to follow through.

Commentary 4 — Gold; the metal prized by all peoples throughout recorded history. Unless the disk, sheet, plate, or chain you buy of this metal is guaranteed to have a very high purity you will find it useless for your magical purpose. Humans are not the only ones who prize this metal above all others. Those intelligent forces and disembodied spirits the magician works with are as fond of it as are we—or perhaps, even more so. However, since it is extremely difficult to obtain any gold object in 24 karat weight, the magician's best source is a wholesale jewelry store or even a goldsmith who sells gold disks, medallions, plates, etc., or who can make a special object of your own design for you. 18 karat gold works extremely well in magical operations, as you will find out for yourself if you have not already done so. Karat weights below this are very questionable, and I do not recommend you even think of anything less than an 18 karat weight.

As for myself, I use—once again—the World Wide Web. There I have found companies that sell 'Placer Gold,' which is the term used for gold that has been precipitated from the original gold ore. It appears as tiny, thin, oblong slivers, dark brown in color, that resemble the color of coffee beans. After procuring it, I simply melt the tiny gold slivers down and pour the metal into a warm, stainless steel mold, thereby literally making my own virgin medallion, disk, or plate. And it is 99.99% pure gold, and as close to pure 24 karat gold as can be attained. Thus I am not only assured that the object is pure gold, but more importantly, I know it is virgin in nature—as the results of the magical work done with it have borne out.

Commentary 5 — As you know by now, in the case of all metals, they must be as pure as possible—and of course, must be virgin in nature. Once again, this means they must never have been used for any other purpose. Now, the attentive reader might raise the following question at this point, "Why is a lead, tin, stainless steel, or even a gold medallion or plate that I buy ready-made from an occult or other supplier 'virgin,' when the lead used in making a fishing sinker is not? After all, the lead used in the fishing sinker was used for the 'purpose' of making it into a sinker. This new lead, tin, steel, or gold disk I'm buying must also have been used or produced for a previously determined purpose, right? I mean, the metal was used to produce the disk or plate in the first place and was intended for some reason, or else it wouldn't have been made! So what's the difference? Am I being too picky here and carrying this thing too far or what?"

Good question! And no, you are not being too picky or carrying this thing too far. In fact, you have carried it as far as it should be carried, but which most who practice so-called New Age 'Magick' haven't even thought about. Ironically, in practical working, you can most certainly get away with using a commercially produced disk, plate, medallion, etc., **IF** it is of a high metal purity. Why is this? Frankly, I don't know. What I do know from my own experience, is that the magical results obtained between buying a disk, plate, medallion, etc., of some metal, and of producing the object myself from the raw metal, are greater than the difference between day and night. I thought about questioning a number of demons I have evoked to physical manifestation about this. But always other priorities took over after the manifestation occurred, and I followed through with those other pressing matters and not with a question that was more of a curious nature.

Theoretically, you are correct. Such a metallic object is not truly virgin, and for the reason you stated. That is why I have taken to producing my own metal objects as explained above. Unlike the merchant or supply house that sells these items for the 'purpose' of another's self-beautification or for some material end, when I pour mine, they are made for one and only one purpose: for the magical operations in which they are to be used. Hence I am guaranteed of their purity *and* of their virgin nature. There is something a little deeper in my argument here, and I advise the reader to reread this section several times, and to think on it most carefully.

Nevertheless, if you choose to use supply houses of one type or another for copper—or for any other metal, of course—it might surprise you to know that high grade (high purity) copper is readily available from two commercial sources: the jewelry industry (of course) and from the electrical and plumbing industry! For these industries have building codes and material requirements to ensure that the rate of fluid flow and its composition—in the case of the plumbing trade—and electrical conduction and performance in the case of the electrical industry—will be safe for the fluid pressures and electrical currents carried by their products. They are also strict in enforcing these codes, to enable Fluid Mechanic and Hydraulic Engineers, as well as Electrical Engineers, to uniformly design according to modern commercial and residential requirements. In effect, visiting a local plumbing or electrical supply house can easily give you the copper dish, plate, or other object that you can then fashion into a sigil base or medallion for magical working. And you can be certain of its high grade purity—but for copper only—in this instance.

Commentary 6 — There has been much dispute over the meaning of this metal-type classically assigned to the planet Mercury. That is, a dispute since the New Age dawned upon us. For it is clear from such ancient and medieval sources as: *Collectanea Chemica*[34]; *A Compendium of Alchemical Processes*[35]; *The Golden Chain of Homer, Parts 1 and 2*[36]; *Compound of Alchemy/Liber Secretissimus/The Marrow of Alchemy*[37]; *Theatrum Chemicum Britannicum*[38]; *The Hermetic and Alchemical Writings of Paracelsus*[39]; *The Triumphal Chariot of Antimony*[40]; and *Last Will and Testament of Basil Valentine*[41]; that Medieval magicians knew what this 'metal' was. And this superior knowledge of Alchemy was added to their magical practices in order to work with the powerful forces of Hod and Mercury.

But in today's age, we are forced to consider what is 'Fixed Mercury'? Many New Age ideas have been advanced in an attempt to 'clarify' and 'define' this, but none have succeeded. And I define the New Age as that form of stylized Western Magic—and its numerous current offshoots—that arose immediately after the breakup of the original London-based Isis-Urania Golden Dawn Temple in 1900. Some of those ideas advanced include:

• Waiting for the planet Mercury to appear in a 'Fixed' zodiacal sign, and then using the metal assigned to the planetary ruler of that sign as the 'Fixed Mercury' of the planet Mercury. For example. According to this fanciful New Age view, one could wait until Mercury enters the Zodiacal Sign of Taurus and then—according to this scheme—use copper, the metal of Venus, the planet that rules Taurus, as the 'Fixed Mercury' for their magical operation. Other imaginative notions include—

• Using a 'mixed metal' for 'Fixed Mercury,' such as copper and silver, silver and mercury, or even brass, an alloy of copper and zinc. Even in Regardie's personal 1910 edition of the *Goetia* that he gave me many years ago, the recommendation is found that the metal to be used for Fixed Mercury is, "Probably the Seals of...Presidents [should be made] in mixture either of Copper and Silver, or of Silver and Mercury..."[42]

As a result of so much confusion, I suspect that many demons of the *Goetia,* for instance, have been left severely alone, when it comes to Evocation to Physical Manifestation. Or, if attempts were made to evoke these beings using the New Age schemes discussed above, either no results, negative results, partial results—or very possibly when working with the demons of Mercury—disastrous results were produced, and always with the massive Slingshot Effect which I discussed at length in *Ceremonial Magic and the Power of Evocation.*

No, the long and short of it is that 'Fixed Mercury' is a magnificent orange, transparent, **glass**, that is prepared in an alchemical manner only. It is made by first 'fluxing' and then heating Antimony Trioxide to a certain high temperature—which is actually well above 1,000 degrees *Celsius*, not Fahrenheit, the temperature scale we normally employ. This heating process requires (today) a very specially made Muffle Furnace. The molten glass is then poured onto a warm steel plate. A round mold can be used to produce a circular piece of the glass if so desired, or a further occult correspondence of Mercury can be added to the 'metal's' final design, by pouring the molten glass into an eight-sided geometrical polygon called an Octagon.

So what is the serious magician to do if he or she wants to work with the Mercurial forces, whether in Invocational, Talismanic, or Evocational magic? Invocation and Talismanic magic yield well to the use of orange colored paper, inks, etc., or woods that are typically associated and ascribed to Hod and Mercury. These can be utilized safely and generally produce excellent results. However, I caution the reader not to attempt the evocation to physical manifestation of a spiritual intelligence with these common devices. If these are employed, I cannot begin to tell you of the magnitude of the Slingshot Effect you will bring upon yourself. And it will be negative in the extreme.

I am planning on writing *a three volume set in Practical Laboratory Alchemy*, as it was taught to me by the late Frater Albertus (Dr. Albert Richard Riedel) of the former Paracelsus Research Society in Salt Lake City, Utah, during my seven years of in-residence study there under his tutelage. In those books, I will go into great detail as to how—among many other things—a simple Muffle Furnace can be built that will allow the magician to pour not only the orange glass of antimony required for mercurial evocations, but indeed how all of the seven colors of the glass of antimony can be alchemically prepared, with each color corresponding to the appropriate planet in question. The reader will find that these different colored glasses of antimony give *far superior* magical results, whether they are applied to the magic of Invocation, Talismanic, or in Evocation to Physical Manifestation. I have presented this somewhat lengthy Commentary as something for the serious magician to carefully consider.

Commentary 7 — For those who prefer to use ready-made silver disks, plates, rings, etc., in their magical work, it is best to purchase them from a fine jewelry store or occult supply house. Always specify that the item be made of *Sterling Silver*, and that of the *highest quality*. The results obtained using such high grade silver—whether in Invocational Magic, Talismanic Magic, or in Evocation to Physical Manifestation, are always striking. Throughout my (now) forty-two years of magical practice, I have used both ready-made metallic devices such as those just described above, as well as those that were of my own creation.

Once again, while the results I obtained from high quality, purchased rings, disks, plates, etc., have been very, very good, I found that the results attained when I produced my own metallic devices were—in each and every case—always nothing short of spectacular. As in so many things in life, you get out of something—anything—exactly what you put into it. Be guided accordingly.

II. Planetary Correspondences Assigned to Various Suffumigations

In Old System Magic, the terms "Suffumigations" or "Perfumes" are used to indicate those odiferous substances—herbs, tree woods, plants, gums, resins, even fruits and vegetables—that are used as offerings to the disincarnate spirit intelligences being called upon in one of the branches of magic, and which aid in their materialization. A classic example of this can be found in the *Heptameron* of the *Fourth Book of Occult Philosophy* ascribed to Henry Cornelius Agrippa.

Since I do not agree with any of the trite attitudes and terminologies of the New Age, I do not use the term incense, as its technical definition is much too narrow to account for the breadth and scope of items that are truly used in the magical arts and sciences, as given above. The following lists—while not extensive by any means—are yet highly functional, in that most of the substances are relatively easy to obtain. Additionally, in the case of those that are not readily available locally, the URL I provided earlier will put the magician in touch with a great many occult suppliers, many of whom carry various herbs, including the exotic types. This will enable the practitioner to lay hold of those materials without too much difficulty.

† Suffumigations of the Planet Saturn

Aconite — Amaranth — Beech — Barley — Bistort — Blue Bottle — Boneset — Buckthorn — Clown's Woundwort — Comfrey — Crosswort — Dodder of Thyme — Elm Tree (the bark, leaves, and flowers are all of use in magic) — Fern (also called, "Royal Fern") — Fluxweed — Fumitory — Gall Oak — Gladwin — Goutweed — Hawkweed — Heart's Ease — Hellebore (Black) — Hellebore (White) — Holly — Horsetail — Ivy — Knapweed — Knapwort (or Harshweed) — Knottgrass — Lady's Slipper — Morning Glory

— Mullein (both Black and 'Great') — Myrrh — Patchouly —
Poplar (both Black and White) — Quince Tree — Red Beet —
Saffron (both Wild and Meadow) — Scullcap — Shepherd's Purse
— Solomon's Seal — Willow Herb   .

† Suffumigations of the Planet Jupiter

Agrimony — Alexanders (also known as "Wild Parsley") — Anise
— Asparagus — Balm — Bilberry — Borage — Chervil —
Chestnut Tree (Bark, Fruit, and Leaves) — Cinquefoil — Clove —
Dandelion — Dock — Dog's Grass — Fir Tree (also known as
"Spruce Fir") — Hart's Tongue — Houseleek — Hyssop —
Linden — Lime Tree — Lungwort — Maple Tree (the bark and
leaves are used for magical purposes) — Meadowsweet — Oak
Tree (the bark, fruit, and leaves are used for magical purposes) —
Nutmeg — Sage (the "Common Garden" Sage only) — Water
Betony — Witch Grass — White Beet — Wood Betony

† Suffumigations of the Planet Mars

Arssmart — Asafetida — Asarabacca — Barberry — Basil — Black
Horehound — Blood Root — Briony (or Bryony) — Butcher's
Broom (also referred to as simply, "Broom") — Chives —
Common Pine — Coriander — Crow Foot — Dragon's Blood —
Eve Weed — Flaxweed — Galangal — Garlic — Gentian — Goat's
Thorn — Hawthorn — High John the Conqueror — Honeysuckle
— Hops — Hound's Tongue — Leek — Lesser Celandine —
Madder — Masterwort — Mustard — Nettle — Onion — Pepper
— Peppermint — Pine — Prickly Ash — Radish — Savine — Sloe
— Tarragon — Tobacco — Woodruff — Wormwood

† Suffumigations of Sol

Acacia — Angelica — Ash Tree — Bay Tree — Benzoin — Burnet
— Butter Bur — Cedar — Celandine — Centaury — Chamomile
— Cinnamon — Corn Feverfew — Eyebright — Frankincense —
Goldenseal — Heliotrope — Juniper — Lovage — Mastic —
Mistletoe — Olive — Peony — Red Sandalwood (not white) —
Rosemary — Rue Saffron (different from Meadow and Wild
Saffron. The proper botanical name of this type of Saffron is
"Crocus Sativus") — St. John's Wort — Sun Dew — Sunflower —
Tormentil — Walnut

† Suffumigations of the Planet Venus

Alder (both Black and Common) — Birch Tree — Blackberry (fruit, leaves, root, and stems have magical usage) — Catmint — Colt's Foot — Columbine — Cowslip — Daisy — Dittany of Crete — Elder — Feverfew (not "Corn" Feverfew which is under the dominion of Sol) — Figwort — Fleabane — Foxglove — Golden Rod — Gooseberry — Lady's Mantle — Mayweed — Mint (both Peppermint and Spearmint. They are *not* under Mercury, as some current books have classified them) — Moneywort — Motherwort — Mugwort — Pennyroyal — Pennywort — Periwinkle — Ragwort — Silverweed — Sorrel (all types, including Common, Sheep's and Wood) — Strawberries — Tansy Thyme — Vervain — Wheat — White Dittany — Wood Aloes — Wood Sage

† Suffumigations of the Planet Mercury

Agaric — Almond — Bittersweet — Caraway — Carrot (Wild) — Dill — Dog's Mercury — Elecampane — Fennel — Fenugreek — Fern (Brake only. "Royal Fern" falls under Saturn—see above suffumigations for Saturn) — Flax — Goat's Rue — Hazel Tree (all parts—fruit, leaves, root, and wood, are under the government of Mercury, not the Sun or any other planet, as some New Age books insist) — Horehound — Hound's Tongue — Lavender — Lily of the Valley — Licorice (again, this plant falls under Mercury, New Age contrivances notwithstanding) — Maiden Hair — Mandrake — Marjoram — Mastic — Mulberry Tree — Parsley — Savory — Senna — Southernwood — Storax — Trefoil — Valerian

† Suffumigations of the Luna

Adder's Tongue — Aloes — Bladder Wrack — Chickweed — Clary — Cucumber — Dog Rose — Great Burnet — Jasmine — Lady's Smock — Lettuce — Lily — Lotus — Mercury (herb) — Moonwort — Poppy — Pumpkin — Rattle Grass — Small Burnet — Speedwell — Stone Crop — Wall Flower — Willow Tree — Wintergreen — Wooly Faverel — Yellow Flag

III. Zodiacal Correspondences Assigned to Certain Suffumigations

Commentary 8 — Due to broadband zodiacal effects, the various mechanisms through which those effects are manifested, and the multiplicity of a given plant's nature, do not *necessarily* expect to see a correspondence between the plants assigned to a given planet and a given Zodiacal Sign. For example: Wood Betony is assigned to the planet Jupiter. Yet, it also corresponds to the Sign of Aries, which is ruled by Mars.

Aries — Dragon's Blood and Wood Betony
Taurus — Lovage, White Dittany, and Wood Aloes
Gemini — Almond, Dog's Mercury, Goat's Rue
Cancer — Agrimony, Black Alder, Hyssop, and Water Betony
Leo — Angelica, Celandine, Eyebright, Rue, and St. John's Wort
Virgo — Fennel, Fenugreek, Maiden Hair, and Valerian
Libra — Dittany of Crete, Mayweed, and Silverweed
Scorpio — Basil, Blood Root, Galangal, High John the Conqueror
Sagittarius — Borage, Dandelion, Lady's Smock, and Hyssop
Capricorn — Aconite, Buckthorn, Butcher's Broom, and Fumitory
Aquarius — Beech, Barley, Fluxweed, Gall Oak, Holly
Pisces — Alder (Common, only), Maple Tree, Nutmeg, and Oak Tree

IV. Certain Suffumigations Assigned to the Elements

Commentary 9 — As is common in these matters, please observe that—once again—a correspondence between a given herb or plant, its planetary attribution and its Elemental correspondence, are not necessarily congruent. For instance. In the case of the Element Air, we find that the ancients assigned the plant Acacia to it. Yet properly speaking, Acacia falls under the dominion of Sol.

Air — Acacia, Agrimony, Caraway, Hazel, and Lily of the Valley
Earth — Barley, Fumitory, Horehound, Mugwort, and Wheat
Water — Chamomile, Chickweed, Lettuce, Tansy, Wood Aloes
Fire — Basil, Blood Root, Damiana, Dragon's Blood, Tobacco

V. Certain Suffumigations Assigned to the Sephiroth

Kether — Ambergris
Chokmah — Musk
Binah — Lily and Myrrh

Chesed — Cedar
Geburah — Dragon's Blood, Tobacco, and Nettle
Tiphareth — Frankincense and Gum Olibanum
Netzach — Benzoin and White Sandalwood
Hod — Storax
Yesod — Jasmine
Malkuth — Dittany of Crete

Commentary 10 — Although assigned to Venus, Dittany of Crete is also attributed to Malkuth, due to its heavy, earthy quality. It is typically used in Evocation to Physical Manifestation to provide a slow-moving, dense smoke in which the spirit entity can effect the *first phase* of its manifestation.

VI. Suffumigations or Perfumes Assigned to the Twenty-Two Paths of the Tree of Life

Commentary 11 — There has been much disagreement in magical circles for many centuries regarding a seemingly minor point of Kabbalah when it comes to the assignment of jewels, suffumigations (perfumes), plants, and even colors associated with the Paths. These contrary views can be found in the earliest Kabbalistic writings, wherein one author felt a certain correspondence was called for in a given instance, and another author leaned toward still another correspondence. Over time, any given dispute attracted its adherents, who then went on to add further correspondences. In turn, these new attributions attracted other adherents as well as opponents.

You can see the problem. Just as in geometrical progression where $2 \times 2 \times 2 \times 2 \times 2...n$ will soon produce an astronomical number, this human trend to agree and disagree grew out of hand. As a result, by the 1930's with Golden Dawn-type magic embedding itself deeply in the Western psyche, a filtering process eventually took over, and a set of attributions arose from the most prominent writers of that time. Namely, Aleister Crowley and Israel Regardie. Their Kabbalistic assignments eventually became the 'classical' attributions typically used in Western Magic today.

So what does all of this mean for us, in terms of laying a sound subconscious state of subjective synthesis and applying it through our daily magical working? Just this. When a Path is assigned a perfume and a plant as well, both are interchangeable when used to contact that Path, as in, for example, Path Working Magic. In reality, neither one is 'better' than the other, or has more 'power.' Both have their place, by virtue of that same type of broadband effect. That is, for a given Path, the use of a given plant over its perfume, or its perfume over its plant, simply means the magician is tuning in to a particular frequency that is characteristic of a particular Path. Much in the same way we tune a radio dial to get a particular radio station we are interested in.

There is also the human element to consider here. Each of us feel and perceive differently a complex composite of an infinite number of physical, physiological, psychological, and psychic factors. And this does not even take into consideration that intuitive leaning toward either a plant or a perfume of a particular Path, which turns out to be no small consideration itself. Thus, one practitioner may find that the perfume of certain Paths—or of all Paths, for that matter—give him or her the best results. Another may find the opposite to be true for them—that the plant assigned to a given Path—or for all Paths—are what yield the best results in their case. As is the case in all Practical Kabbalah—that is, in all Practical Magic—the individual must *experiment* to determine what is best for him or her.

Finally, the reader will notice I have listed only the suffumigations proper for each Path. Why did I not also list the jewel, magical weapon, etc.? Because these other concerns are—according to my experience and the experience of so many whom I have taught—secondary at best, in contacting a Path and in directing its energy. If the individual is so disposed toward a more complete understanding of these other correspondences, I recommend the study of *The Tree of Life*[43] and *A Garden of Pomegranates*[14], both written by Israel Regardie. If the reader then studies *The Mystical Qabalah*[16] by Dion Fortune before launching into the more complex writing of those others found in the recommended reading list, he or she will be well on their way to making sense of it all, which is a process that will—I sincerely trust—take decades to arrive at.

Path Number Eleven, connecting Kether and Chokmah—
Perfume: Galbanum   *Plant*: Acacia

Path Number Twelve, connecting Kether and Binah—
Perfume: Mastic   *Plant*: Vervain

Path Number Thirteen, connecting Kether and Tiphareth—
Perfume: Aloes   *Plant*: Mercury (herb) and Wintergreen

Path Number Fourteen, connecting Chokmah and Binah—
Perfume: Rose   *Plant*: Myrtle

Path Number Fifteen, connecting Chokmah and Tiphareth—
Perfume: Dragon's Blood and Wood Betony   *Plant*: Geranium

Path Number Sixteen, connecting Chokmah and Chesed—
Perfume: Storax   *Plant*: Mallow

Path Number Seventeen, connecting Binah and Tiphareth—
Perfume: Lavender and Lily of the Valley   *Plant*: Orchid

Path Number Eighteen, connecting Binah and Geburah—
Perfume: Hyssop and Black Alder   *Plant*: Lotus

Path Number Nineteen, connecting Chesed and Geburah—
Perfume: Olibanum   *Plant*: Sunflower

Path Number Twenty, connecting Chesed to Tiphareth—
Perfume: Valerian   *Plant*: Narcissus

Path Number Twenty-One, connecting Chesed and Netzach—
Perfume: Saffron   *Plant*: Hyssop and the Oak Tree

Path Number Twenty-Two, connecting Geburah and Tiphareth—
Perfume: Galbanum   *Plant*: Aloe

Commentary 12 — There is no error here regarding the perfume of this Path. Both Path Twenty-Two and Path Eleven share this same odiferous perfume.

Path Number Twenty-Three, connecting Geburah and Hod—
Perfume: Myrrh   *Plant*: Lotus

Path Number Twenty-Four, connecting Tiphareth and Netzach—
Perfume: Galangal   *Plant*: Blood Root

Path Number Twenty-Five, connecting Tiphareth and Yesod—
Perfume: Agrimony, Borage, and Hyssop   *Plant*: Maple Tree

Commentary 13 — As before, there is no error in the listing of Hyssop as the perfume for this Path, even though its magical properties also list it as the perfume for Path Eighteen. Notice also, that for Path Twenty-One, Hyssop is listed as the Plant of that Path.

Path Number Twenty-Six, connecting Tiphareth and Hod—
Perfume: Mush   *Plant*: Buckthorn

Path Number Twenty-Seven, connecting Netzach and Hod—
Perfume: Pepper   *Plant*: Anise

Commentary 14 — Notice that Anise is the herb attributed to this Path. It is actually a herb related to the carrot family, which is attributed to the planet Mercury. Yet, owing to the Yetziratic Title given this Path, "The Natural Intelligence," the herb finds a naturally expressive correspondence to the Path in being assigned as its Plant. Equally, we find from Kabbalistic Theory that this Path takes the astrological attribution of Mars, which finds its expression in the perfume Pepper, which is assigned to that planet. All in all, we find that the Kabbalah does take into account those multi-faceted and diverse ideas upon which the universe is founded.

Path Number Twenty-Eight, connecting Netzach to Yesod—
Perfume: Galbanum   *Plant*: Olive

Commentary 15 — Once more we find Galbanum being assigned to yet a third Path. In this case, the Twenty-Eight Path of Tzaddi, thereby sharing it with Path Number Eleven and Path Number Twenty-Two. Since this twenty-eighth Path connects the two distinctly feminine planets of Venus and the Moon, we find a further correspondence in it when it is compared with Path Number Eleven, whose Elemental attribution is that of Air. The reader would do well to think on this.

Path Number Twenty-Nine, connecting Netzach and Malkuth—
Perfume: Nutmeg   *Plant*: Maple Tree

Path Number Thirty, connecting Hod and Yesod—
Perfume: Cinnamon   *Plant*: Heliotrope and Laurel

Path Number Thirty-One, connecting Hod and Malkuth—
Perfume: Olibanum   *Plant*: Red Poppy

Commentary 16 — The reader may have noticed that the perfume of this Path takes the same perfume as that assigned to Path 19. Olibanum, referred to as "Incense in Tears"[44] is actually a resinous gum whose habitat is Arabia. It is a synonym for Frank-incense, a substance that comes under the rule of the Sun.

I cannot recommend highly enough a supplier of rare and exotic plants, perfumes, gums and resins with whom I have done business with for years. This individual is extremely helpful, and will assist the practitioner in his needs. His store can be found on the World Wide Web at:

http://www.alchemy-works.com

Path Number Thirty-Two, connecting Yesod and Malkuth—
Perfume: Hellebore   *Plant*: Ash

Epilogue

In this book, I have attempted not only to show that there is a vast difference between the gun slinging approach of the New Age and legitimate Western Magic, but have done my best to show just what that difference is, and how it works. Western Magic—as typically defined by Golden Dawn-type doctrines, ritual, and ceremonial practices—is indeed a powerful and workable system of magic when practiced correctly, that is, with intelligence, research, and plain hard work.

From Kabbalistic Analysis to the technique of Path Working Magic I advocate herein, the contemporary magician will find that these devices truly do make a powerful difference when applied to his or her own personal magical efforts. And that difference, when applying them to Western magical practices, will be the difference between receiving partial results from those practices, and full results—and the latter without the Slingshot Effect that none of us either want or need.

This being the third book I have written in Magic, I have found—as all authors find regardless of their field of expertise—that critics abound. Both those that enjoy the books and offer constructive criticism, personal stories and insights, to those few who just refuse to listen to anything but the going orthodox, dogmatic line of their 'New Age' miasma.

To the first group, I wish to express my sincerest gratitude for the helpful and insightful feedback you have provided. An author is only as his good as his reading public, and to those whom I have helped through my writing, I can only promise you that I will continue to do all I can to help you iron out your own personal, harmoniously eclectic system of magic, while building up your subconscious state of subjective synthesis to such a degree, that the day will come when you will be able to operate magic without the formal ritual trappings that are so necessary now.

183

To the latter group of critics, I offer my condolences. I am sure it will take many, many more trips to your favorite bookstore—always looking for that secret book that will give it all without work—before you find out the truth about yourself in general, and magic in particular. The fault, dear Brutus, lies not in our stars, but in ourselves, that we are underlings.

References

To The Reader

1. Lisiewski, Joseph C., Ph.D. *Ceremonial Magic & The Power of Evocation*. New Falcon Publications, Tempe, Arizona. 2004.
2. Lisiewski, Joseph C., Ph.D. *Kabbalistic Cycles & the Mastery of Life*. New Falcon Publications, Tempe, Arizona. 2004.
3. Agrippa, Henry Cornelius of Nettesheim. *Three Books of Occult Philosophy*. Translated by James Freake, edited and annotated by Donald Tyson. Llewellyn Publications, St. Paul, Minnesota. 1993.
4. Agrippa, Henry Cornelius. *Fourth Book of Occult Philosophy*. Kessinger Publishing Company, Montana.

Chapter One

5. Kaplan, Aryeh, translator and commentary. *Sefer Yetzirah. The Book of Creation in Theory and Practice,* revised ed. Samuel Weiser, Inc., York Beach, Maine. 1997, pg. xi.
6. Regardie, Israel. *The Complete Golden Dawn System of Magic*. New Falcon Publications, Tempe, Arizona. 2003.
7. Griffin, David. *The Ritual Magic Manual. A Complete Course in Practical Magic*. Golden Dawn Publishing, Beverly Hills and Stockholm. 1999.

Chapter Two

8. Regardie, Israel. *The Golden Dawn. An Account of the Teachings, Rites and Ceremonies of the Order of the Golden Dawn*. 2nd ed. (Volumes One and Two under one cover.) Distributed by

Llewellyn Publications, St. Paul, Minnesota. 1969. Vol. I, pg. 109.

9. Regardie, Israel. *Twelve Steps to Spiritual Enlightenment.* Sangreal Foundation, Inc., Dallas, Texas. 1969.

10. Regardie, Israel. *The Original Account of the Teachings, Rites and Ceremonies of the Hermetic Order of The Golden Dawn.* 6th ed., revised and enlarged. Llewellyn Publications, St. Paul, Minnesota. 1995.

Chapter Three

11. Lewis, H. Spencer, F.R.C., Ph.D. *Self Mastery and Fate with the Cycles of Life.* The Rosicrucian Press, Ltd., San Jose, California. 1st ed. 1929, 26th ed. 1971.

12. Agrippa, Henry Cornelius of Nettesheim. *Three Books of Occult Philosophy.* Translated by James Freake, edited and annotated by Donald Tyson. Llewellyn Publications, St. Paul, Minnesota. 1993. pg. 371.

13. Ibid.

Chapter Four

14. Regardie, Israel. *A Garden of Pomegranates. An Outline of the Qabalah.* 2nd ed. Llewellyn Publications, St. Paul, Minnesota. 1994.

15. Matt, Daniel C. *The Essential Kabbalah—The Heart of Jewish Mysticism.* Castle Books, New Jersey, 1997 ed.

16. Fortune, Dion. *The Mystical Qabalah.* Ernest Benn Limited, London. 1957.

17. Kaplan, Aryeh, translator and commentary. *Sefer Yetzirah. The Book of Creation. In Theory and Practice.* rev. ed., Samuel Weiser, Inc., York Beach, Maine. 1997.

18. Scholem, Gershom, editor. *Zohar. The Book of Splendor. Basic Readings from the Kabbalah.* Schocken Books, New York. 1977.

19. Reuchlin, Johann. *De Arte Cabalistica. On the Art of the Kabbalah.* University of Nebraska Press, Lincoln, Nebraska. 1993.

20. Levi, Eliphas. *The Book of Splendours. The Inner Mysteries of Qabalism. Its Relationship to Freemasonry, Numerology, and Tarot.* Samuel Weiser, Inc., York Beach, Maine. 1984.

21. Levi, Eliphas. *The Mysteries of the Qabalah or Occult Agreement of the Two Testaments.* Samuel Weiser, Inc., York Beach, Maine. 2000.

22. Waite, Arthur Edward. *The Holy Kabbalah. A Mystical Interpretation of the Scriptures.* Carol Publishing Group. 1995.

23. Greer, John Michael. *The New Encyclopedia of the Occult.* Llewellyn Publications, St. Paul, Minnesota. 2003.

24. Fortune, Dion. *The Mystical Qabalah.* Ernest Benn Limited, London. 1957. pg. 197

Chapter Six

25. Waite, Arthur Edward. *The Pictorial Key to the Tarot.* Weiser Books, York Beach, Maine. 2000. (Original edition 1910.)

26. Mathers, S.L. MacGregor. *The Tarot: Its Occult Significance, Use in Fortune-Telling, and Method of Play.* Sq. 16 mo., London, 1888.

27. Levi, Eliphas. *The Magical Ritual of the Sanctum Regnum, Interpreted by the Tarot Trumps.* W. Wynn Westcott, translator. London, 1896.

28. *The Spiritual Exercises of St. Ignatius.* Catholic Publication Society. Kessinger Publishing Company, Montana.

29. Ibid. pg. vii

30. Ibid, pg. 3

31. Ibid. pg. ix

32. Ibid. pg. xi

33. Ibid. pg. xii

Chapter Seven

34. Philalethes; Eirenaeus, Dr. Francis Anthony, George Starkey, Sir George Ripley, and Anonymous Unknown. *Collectanea Chemica: Being Certain Select Treatises on Alchemy and Hermetic Medicine.* Kessinger Publishing Company, Montana.

35. *A Compendium of Alchemical Processes. Extracted from the Writings of: Glauber, Basil Valentine, and other Adepts.* Kessinger Publishing Company, Montana.

36. Kirchweger, Anton, editor. *The Golden Chain of Homer as Part 1 and Part 2,* being Volumes Two and Three of the Alchemical Manuscript Series published by AMORC (Ancient and Mystical Order Rosae Crucis, Inc.) San Jose, CA. 1993.

37. Ripley, George. [1591] *Compound of Alchemy/Liber Secretissimus/ The Marrow of Alchemy,* being Volume Six of the Alchemical Manuscript Series published by AMORC (Ancient and Mystical Order Rosae Crucis, Inc.) San Jose, CA. 1993.

38. Ashmole, Elias. [1651] *Treatrum Chemicum Britannicum.* Kessinger Publishing Company, Montana.

39. Paracelsus. *The Hermetic and Alchemical Writings of Aureolus Phillippus Theophratus Bombast of Hohenheim, called Paracelsus, the Great.* Kessinger Publishing Company, Montana.

40. Valentinus, Basilius. [1685] *The Triumphal Chariot of Antimony.* Kessinger Publishing Company, Montana.

41. Valentine, Basil. *Last Will and Testament,* being Volume Fourteen of the Alchemical Manuscript Series published by AMORC (Ancient and Mystical Order Rosae Crucis, Inc.) San Jose, CA. 1993.

42. *Goetia. The Book of the Goetia or The Lesser Key of Solomon the King, by the order of the Second Chief of the Rosicrucian Order.* The Occult Publishing House, Chicago. 1910. pg. 45.

43. Regardie, Israel. *The Tree of Life. A Study in Magic.* Samuel Weiser, Inc. NY. 1971.

44. Mathers, S.L. MacGregor, translator. *The Book of the Sacred Magic of Abramelin the Mage as delivered by Abraham the Jew unto his son Lamech A.D. 1458.* Dover Publications, Inc., NY. 1975. pg. 77.

Recommended Reading List

A Compendium of Alchemical Processes. Extracted from the Writings of: Glauber, Basil Valentine, and other Adepts. Kessinger Publishing Company, Montana.

Agrippa, Henry Cornelius of Nettesheim. *Three Books of Occult Philosophy.* Translated by James Freake, edited and annotated by Donald Tyson. Llewellyn Publications, St. Paul, Minnesota. 1993.

Agrippa, Henry Cornelius. *Fourth Book of Occult Philosophy.* Kessinger Publishing Company, Montana.

Ashmole, Elias. [1651] *Treatrum Chemicum Britannicum.* Kessinger Publishing Company, Montana.

Assagioli, Roberto, M.D. *The Act of Will.* Penguin Books, NY. 1973.

Assagioli, Roberto, M.D. *Psychosynthesis.* Penguin Books, NY. 1976.

Barrett, Francis. *The Magus, or Celestial Intelligencer; being a complete system of Occult Philosophy.* Introduction by Timothy d'Arch Smith (1967). Citadel Press Book. Reprint Samuel Weiser, Inc., York Beach, Maine. 1989.

Brenner, Charles, M.D. *An Elementary Textbook of Psychoanalysis.* Bantam-Doubleday-Dell Publishing Group, Inc., NY. 1995.

Brill, Dr. A.A., editor and translator. *The Basic Writings of Sigmund Freud.* Random House, Inc., NY. 1995.

Campbell, Joseph, editor. *The Portable Jung.* Penguin Books, New York. 1976.

Fortune, Dion. *The Mystical Qabalah.* Ernest Benn Limited, London. 1957.

Freud, Sigmund. *General Psychological Theory. Papers on Metapsychology.* Simon & Schuster, NY. 1997

Freud, Sigmund. *An Outline of Psycho-Analysis.* W.W. Norton & Co., NY. 1989

Freud, Sigmund. *Psychopathology of Everyday Life.* A.A. Brill, translator. Dover Publications, Inc. Mineola, New York. 2003.

Goetia. The Book of the Goetia or The Lesser Key of Solomon the King, by the order of the Second Chief of the Rosicrucian Order. The Occult Publishing House, Chicago. 1910. pg. 45.

Greer, John Michael. *The New Encyclopedia of the Occult.* Llewellyn Publications, St. Paul, Minnesota. 2003.

Griffin, David. *The Ritual Magic Manual. A Complete Course in Practical Magic.* Golden Dawn Publishing, Beverly Hills and Stockholm. 1999.

Horney, Karen, M.D. *Neurosis and Human Growth. The Struggle Toward Self-Realization.* W.W. Norton & Co., New York. 1991.

Horney, Karen, M.D. *Self-Analysis.* W.W. Norton & Co., NY. 1994.

Hyatt, Christopher S., Ph.D. *Undoing Yourself with Energized Meditation and Other Devices.* New Falcon Publications, Tempe, Arizona. 1982.

Hyatt, Christopher S., Ph.D. with Dr. Jack Willis. *The Psychopath's Bible.* New Falcon Publications, Tempe, Arizona. 1994.

Hyatt, Christopher S., Ph.D. and Calvin Iwema. *Energized Hypnosis. A Non-Book for Self Change.* New Falcon Publications. Tempe, Arizona. 2005. (with CDs.)

James, William. *Psychology. The Briefer Course.* Dover Publishing, Inc., NY. 2001.

Jung, Carl G. and M.-L. von Franz, Joseph L. Henderson, Jolande Jacobi, and Aniela Jaffé. *Man and His Symbols.* Bantam Doubleday Dell Publishing Group, Inc., NY. 1968.

Jung, C.G. (1875–1961) *Memories, Dreams, Reflections.* Random House, Inc., NY. 1989.

Jung, C.G. *Psychology of the Unconscious.* Dover Publications, Inc., NY. 2002.

Kaplan, Aryeh, translator and commentary. *Sefer Yetzirah. The Book of Creation in Theory and Practice,* revised ed. Samuel Weiser, Inc., York Beach, Maine. 1997.

Kirchweger, Anton, editor. *The Golden Chain of Homer as Part 1 and Part 2*, being Volumes Two and Three of the Alchemical Manuscript Series published by AMORC (Ancient and Mystical Order Rosae Crucis, Inc.) San Jose, CA. 1993.

Levi, Eliphas. *The Book of Splendours. The Inner Mysteries of Qabalism. Its relationship to Freemasonry, Numerology, and Tarot.* Samuel Weiser, Inc., York Beach, Maine. 1984.

Levi, Eliphas. *The Mysteries of the Qabalah or Occult Agreement of the Two Testaments.* Samuel Weiser, Inc., York Beach, Maine. 2000.

Mathers, S.L. MacGregor, translator. *The Book of the Sacred Magic of Abramelin the Mage as delivered by Abraham the Jew unto his son Lamech A.D. 1458.* Dover Publications, Inc., NY. 1975.

Mathers, S.L. MacGregor, translator. *The Kabbalah Unveiled.* Penguin Books, London. 1991.

Matt, Daniel C. *The Essential Kabbalah—The Heart of Jewish Mysticism.* Castle Books, New Jersey. 1997 ed.

Paracelsus. *The Hermetic and Alchemical Writings of Aureolus Phillippus Theophratus Bombast of Hohenheim, called Paracelsus, the Great.* Kessinger Publishing Company, Montana.

Philalethes, Eirenaeus, Dr. Francis Anthony, George Starkey, Sir George Ripley, and Anonymous Unknown. *Collectanea Chemica: Being Certain Select Treatises on Alchemy and Hermetic Medicine.* Kessinger Publishing Company, Montana.

Regardie, Israel. *The Complete Golden Dawn System of Magic.* New Falcon Publications, Tempe, Arizona. 2003.

Regardie, Israel. *The Original Account of the Teachings, Rites and Ceremonies of the Hermetic Order of The Golden Dawn.* 6th ed., revised and enlarged. Llewellyn Publications, St. Paul, Minnesota. 1995.

Regardie, Israel. *A Garden of Pomegranates. An Outline of the Qabalah.* 2nd ed. Llewellyn Publications, St. Paul, Minnesota. 1994.

Reuchlin, Johann. *On the Art of the Kabbalah.* University of Nebraska Press, Lincoln, Nebraska. 1993.

Ripley, George. [1591] *Compound of Alchemy/Liber Secretissimus/The Marrow of Alchemy,* being Volume Six of the Alchemical Manuscript Series published by AMORC (Ancient and Mystical Order Rosae Crucis, Inc.) San Jose, CA. 1993.

Scholem, Gershom. *Kabbalah. A definitive history of the evolution, ideas, leading figures and extraordinary influence of Jewish mysticism.* Penguin Books, NY. 1978.

Scholem, Gershom, editor. *Zohar. The Book of Splendor. Basic Readings from the Kabbalah.* Schocken Books, NY. 1977.

The Spiritual Exercises of St. Ignatius. Catholic Publication Society. Kessinger Publishing Company, Montana.

Stirling, William. *The Cabala. An Elucidation.* R.C. Abel, editor. Holmes Publishing Group, Edmonds, WA. 1999.

Valentine, Basil. *Last Will and Testament,* being Volume Fourteen of the Alchemical Manuscript Series published by AMORC (Ancient and Mystical Order Rosae Crucis, Inc.) San Jose, CA. 1993.

Valentinus, Basilius. [1685] *The Triumphal Chariot of Antimony.* Kessinger Publishing Company, Montana.

Waite, A.E. *The Holy Kabbalah. A Mystical Interpretation of the Scriptures.* Carol Publishing Group. 1995.

Westcott, William Wynn (1848–1925). *Collectanea Hermetica Parts 1–10.* Introduction by R.A. Gilbert. Samuel Weiser, Inc., York Beach, Maine. 1998.

Westcott, William Wynn, translator. *Sepher Yetzirah. The Book of Formation with The Fifty Gates of Intelligence & The Thirty-Two Paths of Wisdom.* 4th ed. Holmes Publishing Group, Edmonds, WA. 1996.